World War II
Homefront Collectibles

Price & Identification Guide

Martin Jacobs

Published by

**krause
publications**

700 E. State Street • Iola, WI 54990-0001
Telephone: 715/445-2214

Please, call or write us for our free catalog of antiques and collectibles publications. To place an
order or receive our free catalog, call 800-258-0929. For editorial comment and further information,
use our regular business telephone at (715) 445-2214

Library of Congress Catalog Number: 99-68106
ISBN: 0-87341-853-0

Printed in the United States of America

Tribute

To my father Nathan, my hero, who was spared being a casualty of war to come home and be a great dad and who always told me to do the things I love to do. And to my mother Beatrice, who spared me from a communal baby-sitter during the war, to stay home with me and raised me to be honest and always told me to do the right thing.

Beatrice and Nathan Jacobs in 1942.

Foreword

When America entered Word War II, patriotism soon became a way of life. Everyone was involved in the war-effort in every imaginable way. From the soldiers, sailors, airmen and marines fighting in the mud, water and in the air to the housewives now building aircraft and the kids collecting scrap. We were all involved, we were at WAR and like it or not we were in it to WIN! Sure it meant rationing. We were short of everything. It was all needed for the war. Rubber and gasoline to "Keep'em Rolling" and "Keep'em Flying," steel and aluminum for building the guns and tanks and planes, ships and trucks we so desperately needed. Cotton and wool for uniforms and tents and blankets, leather for boots and packs and more boots. They needed it, and the homefront provided it! This would be a costly war, not only in the cost of human life, but in hard dollars, so it was "BUY WAR BONDS and STAMPS," "SAVE FOR VICTORY!" and "BACK THE ATTACK!"

Our Nation needed fighting men and we gave them our sons, husbands and fathers. Our factories needed workers and we gave them our wives, and mothers. The Red Cross, USO and local hospitals needed volunteers, and we gave them our sisters and daughters. Even our senior citizens went back to work and taught in our schools and watched for enemy aircraft and submarines, taught first aid and patrolled our streets. This was everyone's war.

We may not have been ready for another World War, but it didn't take long for America to mobilize. After his government launched the surprise attack against the U.S. Fleet at Pearl Harbor, Admiral Yamamoto of the Imperial Japanese Navy was right when he said "I fear we have awakened a sleeping tiger." That sleeping tiger would awake and within months be sinking Japan's greatest war ships, knocking "Zeros" out of the sky and dropping bombs on the island of Japan.

We were fighting on two fronts, and it would take an all out effort to win, an effort we were willing, able and eager to do. We forgot our differences. We united as Americans against a common enemy, put our shoulders to the wall, our noses to the grindstone, stuck a "To Hell with Hirohito" pin on our overalls and started car pooling. We produced more war materials than any country had ever produced in the shortest period of time. But the thing we can be most proud of is that the homefront supported and produced the best trained, best fed, best paid and best cared for fighting man the world has ever seen. And, just like in those great old movies, good did triumph over evil, the villains were defeated, and the handsome and victorious heroes finally returned home to the unsung heroes of the homefront.

—*Martin S. Jacobs*

Table of Contents

Introduction

For me, collecting Word War II homefront memorabilia has been a treasure hunt like no other. I know that there is that special item, that piece that I don't have, the best one anywhere just waiting for me to find in that next auction, on the Internet, in that interesting shop or at the flea market or garage sale, it's there and it will soon be mine!

I began collecting homefront memorabilia in 1946 at the tender age of 3 when my dad, a Word War II veteran, presented me with his very own dog tags. Little did he know that more than 50 years later and thousands of wonderful items, they would still be my favorite. I really don't remember San Francisco during those years with the all the men and women in their smart looking uniforms, the flags flying on Market Street, the spectacular big band music and, of course, the rationing, the air raid drills the constant threat of the Japanese submarine surfacing under the Golden Gate Bridge and that dreaded telegram from the President.

As a youngster, I soon began collecting everything I could relating to the War. War posters, advertising, bubble gum cards, stickers, patches, spotter planes and model ships. I collected patriotic pins and banners, comic books, flags, victory pins, Remember Pearl Harbor items, newspapers, sweetheart jewelry, anything and everything that was red, white and blue! It made me feel good, proud, important. I was one of the "good guys." Let's face it—we won the war!

Today, collecting homefront memorabilia brings back memories of those special years, when we were the heroes and they were the villains, when our country was united, and we all worked hard, grew our own vegetables, spent at least 10% of our earnings on war bonds and knew that loose lips sunk ships, maybe memories that were really never even there.

I don't know of any other comprehensive homefront collector's book dealing with the thousands of homefront items produced during the war years. It is only with the help of my partner Charles A. Numark, who is the co-owner of this country's largest military antique shop, and our valued and devoted contributors that made this book possible.

World War II Homefront Collectibles is a nostalgic look at this country's wartime patriotic, usually humorous, often outlandish, always fascinating icons. With hundreds of listings with detailed photos and price guide, our book reveals some fairly common and some seldom seen WWII collectibles.

About Pricing

World War II Homefront Collectibles was produced to assist the collectors, as well as dealers, estimate a reasonable value for the Word War II homefront collectibles. Writing this price guide has been a challenge, as I know how important it is to quote the most accurate value possible. After months of research and decades of collecting, I learned one thing: Values are not cast in stone; they are fluid. An item's value is what someone is willing to pay for it. For example, some people collect bottle caps—that's great. I might run into a really good bottle cap but as I don't collect bottle caps, it's book actual value would not apply to me as I would rather spend my money on homefront items. On the other hand, I know that a plaster skunk manufactured in 1942 with Hitler's head in very good condition is worth $225, but not to the person who loves bottle caps.

Understand that values change by every auction and by every sale. If a large quantity of a scarce item is located and sold, the value may go down for a short time. If some new collectors come onto the scene and start buying all the "God Bless America" pieces, prices quickly go up. What you pay depends on where you are doing your shopping, what quantity you are buying and how badly the seller wants to sell the item. The most important factor is how badly you want the piece. The great thing about using this price guide is that you will see items pictured and listed that you never knew existed. You will also be sure that an item valued at $15 is not worth $85, and an item valued at $85 is a steal at $15.

After experiencing the ecstasy of looking over some of the word's great homefront collections and the agony of organizing, categorizing, listing, describing, numbering, typing, reviewing, discussing, changing, reorganizing, re-categorizing, re-listing, re-describing, re-numbering and re-typing, I came up with the most appropriate, most definitive value for each of the more than 2,000 Word War II homefront items listed.

Prices in this guide assume that the item is complete as when it was new and in very good to mint condition. The abbreviation "RWB" stands for "red, white and blue."

Contributors & Collectors

Charles A. Numark

Project Manager/Assistant to Martin Jacobs

Charles A. Numark was born in New York in 1941 to a show-business family. His father was a comedian and spent the closing years of WWII running U.S.O. shows, entertaining the troops. After the war, the family moved to Hollywood; his father was the headliner in Hollywood's biggest stage show, "Earl Carol's Vanities of 1946." Charles loved the movies, and growing up in Hollywood in the 1940s and 1950s was perfect. In 1956, while attending North Hollywood High School, he met Natalie. They were married in 1961 and today live in San Rafael, CA, and have two grown children and two grandchildren.

Charles joined the Air National Guard in 1958 and was honorably discharged after serving seven years as an Air Police Operations Supervisor. Charles re-enlisted into the reserves in 1989 and is a major presently serving as a Brigade Deputy Commander. In 1969, he joined the Los Angeles County Sheriff's Department; for the next 24 years, he served in various positions, ending his law enforcement career as a Criminal Investigator with the Marin County District Attorney's Office.

Charles graduated from Dominican Collage, *summa cum laude*, with a B.A. in Psychology and Administration of Justice and did graduate work at La Verne College and UC-Berkeley, where he earned his teaching credentials.

After retiring in 1992, his interests in the military, coupled with his training in psychology and his law enforcement experiences, lead him to many new enterprises. He has written a screen play dealing with German prisoners of war, designs and leads military tours in Europe, owns a video production company that produces military documentaries, co-owns the country's largest military antique shop, as well as a military museum and antique collective. His Internet page is at: *www.sonic.net/~warstuff*.

Ted Hake

Special thanks to Ted Hake of Hake's Americana and Collectibles, who supplied us with some outstanding photos for this book. Over the years, Ted has shared his expertise by writing 16 reference/price guides covering many subjects. Today, he conducts five annual auctions and offers a wide selection of homefront items. For a free auction catalog write to Hake's Americana and Collectibles, #505, P.O. Box 1444, York, PA 17405; or call (717) 848-1333.

Larry Shedwick

Larry Shedwick is a retired Biology/Life Science teacher of 33 years in Pittsburgh and Ford City, PA. While in grade school, during the war, Larry was one of the Uncle Sam's "Tin Cannoners" and "Jr. Commandos." Larry began collecting when he found a "Remember Pearl Harbor" window decal just like the one his grandfather had on his front door. Today, Larry and his wife Kay present displays and give seminars on World War II homefront and sweetheart jewelry around the country. Larry was instrumental in the production of this book in assisting with photography and historical information.

Thomas Herwer

Thomas Herwer, who calls himself a "war baby," admits he only remembers the blackouts at his parents home in San Pedro, CA. Tom's father was a chief mineman and stationed on the U.S.S. Tern (AM31) during the attack at Pearl Harbor in 1941. Tom's first collectible was a converted shell casing which his dad had turned into a savings bank for Tom. Tom specializes in collecting "Remember Pearl Harbor" mementos and has more than 200 pieces in his collection. Tom served in the U.S. Army and received a degree from California State University. He is retired after 30 years in telecommunications and lives in Hemet, CA.

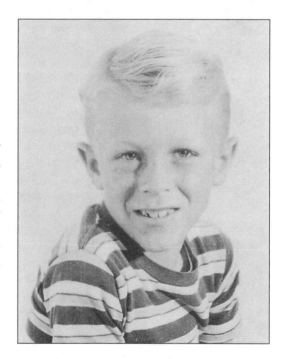

Steve Highlander

Steve developed an early interest in military history while growing up in rural western Missouri. His dad served in Korea, and introduced Steve to all the great war movies, and started him reading about World War II at a young age. Steve began collecting World War II military equipment and uniforms in the 1980s, but has focused primarily on the World War II homefront items since 1990. Steve practices law and lives with his wife and daughter in Austin, TX.

Jimmy Ray Clevenger

Jimmy Ray was born in Kansas City in 1960 and says he has been around the military post all his life. His father served 20 years in the Air Force. Jimmy Ray served 3 years in the Army and has been working for the U.S. Government for the past 15 years. He has collected World War II memorabilia since the 1980s and now specializes in homefront collectibles. For the last 10 years, he has been employed as the golf head coach at the U.S. Military Academy at West Point, NY.

Rick Delgado

Rick was born and raised in Los Angeles. Surrounded by aircraft, shipbuilding and Hollywood studios, World War II stories were always a part of every tour or school field trip. This started a curious young researcher on a seemingly endless journey for more information. After looking for examples of common ration items, his collection has grown to cover almost all aspects of the American homefront. When the opportunity presents itself, he displays some of his photos and items to educate others.

Tim Lowe

As a youngster in Des Moines, IA, Tim said that he grew up leading toy soldiers to victory, sometimes crushing a whole Nazi division with one well placed boulder. Tim's father, Richard Lowe, served in the Navy on the destroyer Escort Carroll (171), from 1942 until the end of the war. Tim began serious collecting in the late-1980s after winning an "Action Yank-E-Tank Army" set in an auction. Today, Tim's focus is on homefront toys and games and he works as a graphic designer. He lives with his wife and three children in St. Charles, MO.

James Lowe

Jim's interest in collecting homefront memorabilia dates back to his childhood. His dad, a post-World War II veteran, along with other family members, shared stories and made frequent trips to the library reading many historical books. Jim's grandfather was at Pearl Harbor prior to the attack, and his great uncle was a bomber mechanic in the Philippines. Today, Jim is a history teacher at Altoona High School in Altoona, PA. He enjoys sharing homefront items from his collection to his students. He specializes in posters, anti-Axis items, buttons, postcards and ration materials.

Dr. Frank Arian

Some of Frank's earliest memories include climbing a 35-foot pile of jungle boots that were just returned from Vietnam at his father's army surplus store. Over the years, Frank developed considerable expertise in combat uniforms from his dad, and has outfitted some of the major war motion pictures such as the "Deer Hunter" and "Uncommon Valor." Today, Frank is an avid homefront collector with more than 1,500 items. He is a graduate of Case Western Reserve University School of Medicine and practices emergency medicine in Bakersfield, Calif.

John D. "Jack" Matthews

Jack was born in 1932. He is a graduate of Holy Cross University and Georgetown University Law School. For three years, served as a Naval Officer on the U.S.S. Tarawa (CVS40). He now serves as the Municipal Court Judge for the Island of Kiawah and Seabrook, SC. Since age 15, Jack has been a collector of toy soldiers, specializing in German composition figures and antique tinplate military toys. Jack's collection is featured in his book, *Toys Go to War.* He is also the author of some 50 articles on his collections. Jack and his wife Merium live in South Carolina and in the mountains of North Carolina.

Nick Snider

A collector since age 7, Nick has always had a desire to collect. He started with pennies. Today, he has a collection of World War I and II "Sweetheart Jewelry" that numbers well over 10,000. Nick is responsible for providing photos from his huge collection which is featured in this book. Nick served as an Infantry Officer and worked 33 years for the United Parcel Service until he retired in 1998 as the Vice President in the corporate office. Nick has two books in publication, *Sweetheart Jewelry* in 1995 and *Sweetheart Jewelry and Collectibles* in 1996, by Schiffer Publishing. Nick has committed the next 10 years to creating "The National Museum of Patriotism" in Atlanta. Nick welcomes any and all support for the museum: the only one of it's kind in America: *www.museumofpatriotism.org.* Nick resides with his wife Betty and three children in Atlanta.

Brian C. Wensel

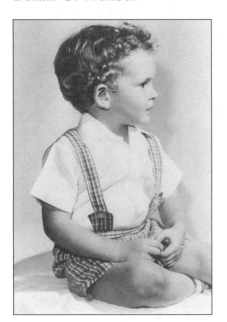

Brian, a native of Philadelphia, has been an avid World War II enthusiast and collector since he was a child. His interest in WWII was sparked by his father who flew 31 combat missions as a waist gunner on a B-17 assigned to the 379th Bomb Group, 8th Air Force. He began collecting WWII military patches in grade school. His collection has continued to grow and evolve the last 30 years to include a variety of WWII memorabilia, with homefront items becoming one of the primary areas of concentration. Brian is vice-president of Production Finance for the Motion Picture Group of Paramount Pictures. He lives in Burbank, CA, with his wife Emily and their Cavalier King Charles Spaniels.

Ken Fleck

Ken has specialized in anti-Axis homefront propaganda since he purchased his first piece in 1987. From then on, his collection has grown, and he displays his award-winning collection at various military shows. Ken's collecting interest actually began at an early age when he took his father's World War II souvenirs to his school to show and tell his friends. But collecting anti-Axis collectibles of Hitler, Tojo and Mussolini, he admits has been the most fun. Ken is a retired ironworker, and today is a full-time auctioneer. Ken resides with his wife Mady in the suburb of Harrisburg, PA.

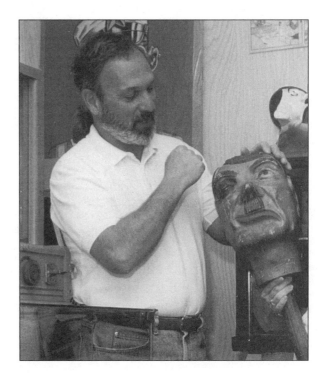

Gejus van Diggele

Gejus, who resides in Hazerswoude in the Netherlands, works from his home-based office as a freelance advertising consultant and copywriter. In addition, Gejus is one of Europe's foremost collector of World War II card games and board games. Gejus has over 1,000 entries in his database of historical information on game collectibles and has done much research on their origins. Since 1994, Gejus has a traveling exhibition called "The War on the Table," with collectibles from 17 countries. His exhibitions have been hosted by museums and galleries in the Netherlands, Belgium, Finland and Germany. He has been a guest speaker with appearances on radio and TV in six countries, including the United States. Gejus can be reached via his e-mail address: *Gejus@euronet.nl.*

Guy Williams

Since Guy was a child, he has had a fascination with the ideals and sentiments from World War II. His grandfather served in the Philippines during the war. At age 9, Guy's parents gave him an Uncle Sam mechanical bank. Sparked by his parent's gift, Guy's first purchase was a chalk destroyer ship war bond bank in which he has increased his collection to over 120 different WWII coin banks. Many of Guy's banks are featured in Chapter 4 "Patriotics." Guy is a graduate of Quincy State College and today works as an accountant for a refuse company and lives in Fowler, IL.

I'd also like to thank and acknowledge the other contributors who helped in the production of this book: Natalie Numark: photos from her collection; Tony Benner: photography; Don Mauer: photography; and Daniel Fermaglich: war gum cards.

About the Author

Martin Jacobs was born in 1943. He was considered a "war baby" (though he did not get a victory celebration at the time of his birth, his dad was away at Army boot camp at Camp White in Oregon). Even today, some 55 years after the war has ended, his dad still recalls his famous 361st Infantry, 91st Division battle cry: "Powder river, Let 'em buck!"

Many newborns born in 1943, a year called "in the mood", were named Victor, Vincent, Valerie, Virginia or Vicky after the celebrated "V" for victory, but his mother had other ideas and named him Martin! His baby carriage was decorated with tiny American flags and his baby crib was adorned in patriotic colors with mobiles of paper fighter planes hanging from above. Even his baby diapers were emblazoned with the letter "V" on the back. His bedroom looked like an Army fort with toy soldiers everywhere, a big poster of Bugs Bunny as a Gunnery Sergeant was tacked to the wall. In his toy box was a round leather kickball with planes, tanks and jeeps painted on it.

It didn't take long for Martin to figure out he was growing up surrounded by the reality of war. When Martin craved sweets, he was told sugar was a rationed item. It was a privilege for Martin to be home with his mother and not stuck with a communal baby-sitter, as most children were because their mothers had to work in the defense plants to earn extra money.

While his mother baked ginger cookies and planted victory gardens, they listened to Walter Winchell talk on the radio about our troops, the U-boats, tail gunners, and our victories. As a war baby, even his first hair cut was an experience to remember. Outside the barbershop, the tall barber pole was actually a painted brass bomb shell.

After all, Martin was a patriot. A blackout warning in his home was to turn off the lights, pull down the shades, then go out on the porch and see nothing but stars, a moon, and a searchlight. There was never a dull moment.

On Sunday's his mother would dress him in his sailor suit and white patent leather shoes. Then his hair was groomed with Kreml Hair Tonic, just like his dad used in the Army. For a day at least, Martin felt like a war hero. It seemed the prevailing feeling was, if dad was a war hero, they all were. Family days were spent at an amusement park where he would take pony rides and enjoy a 5-cent Eskimo Pie, his favorite ice cream bar.

By the time Martin was two, he became a member of the Lone Ranger Victory Corps and wore his pin proudly. Martin's 2nd birthday fell on February 23, 1945, the day our United States flag was raised at Mt. Suribachi, Iwo Jima, in victory. Soon after, American's celebrated V-E Day and V-J Day as the war was officially over. By 1946, Martin's dad came home and traded in his fatigues for civilian clothes. Martin could climb out of bed himself, button his overalls, and color a picture. His dad presented him with his very own first collectible, his Army dog tags which Martin still treasures today.

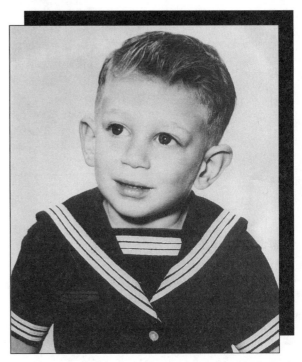

Martin Jacobs 1945.

After graduating high school in 1960, Martin attended City College of San Francisco studying Commercial Art. In 1963 he studied journalism at the University of San Francisco and in 1964 he joined the Army and served until 1970 as a dietary cook at Letterman Hospital in the Presidio of San Francisco. In 1972, he started a mailorder business called "Sports Locker Room", which operated for 21 years. In 1985, he opened the "Sands Hall of Fame Museum" in Las Vegas, Nevada. After retiring in 1993, he was able to concentrate on his first love of collecting-homefront memorabilia.

Today, Martin travels extensively to military and collectible shows looking for that special "Victory" item. As a freelance writer, he's had feature stories on the homefront published in national magazines and newspapers such as *Stars and Stripes, Army and Navy News, Leatherneck, Veterans Press, Military Trader, Antique Trader, Collectors Eye, Toy Trader, Reminisce, Collectit* and others. He was also a major contributor to WWII pictorials, *To Win the War* and *For the Boys.*

Martin resides in San Francisco with his family and is the proud father of 5 children, Jason, Justin, Joshua, Jazmin and Sadie. He would like to hear from his readers and offers free estimates on your homefront collectibles. He can be reached by email: MJacobs784@aol.com or by telephoning 415-6617552 or by writing, P.O. Box 22026, San Francisco, CA. 94122.

Chapter 1
Remember Pearl Harbor

"December 7th, 1941—a date that will live in infamy." From that famous quote came the words "Remember Pearl Harbor!" Let no American forget the surprise attack committed against the United States of America by the forces of the Imperial Japanese Government at our military bases at Pearl Harbor, Hawaii.

Remember Pearl Harbor ("RPH") became the motto of our war against Japan and was echoed across the country on almost anything that could be written on! It was in the newspapers, comic books, envelopes, stickers, window decals and posters. It was "Remember Pearl Harbor" on dishes and glasses and sweaters and banks and toys, plaques and pennants, caps and calendars. It was everywhere!

Today, almost 60 years later, some fortunate collectors still find some of those highly prized momentoes with those fighting words, "Remember Pearl Harbor" on them. Just as powerful today as the words were then, they

Trays, 4-1/4" x 3-1/4", milk glass "RPH" and "Buy U.S. Savings Bonds, 1943 ($75-$95 each).

remind us to "Be Prepared" and "Don't get caught with your pants down." It was "Keep 'em Flying," "Keep 'em Rolling," "God Bless America," "Don't get Axed by the Axis," "Loose Lips Sink Ships," "They're Listening" and many other slogans that kept us alert and angry, but none that had the impact of "Remember Pearl Harbor!"

Item	Value
Banner, felt, "RPH," 11", RWB	$35-$45
Banner, window, silk, "RPH," 9" x 11", gold trim, RWB	$40-$55
Beanie, child's cap, multi-colored, patriotic slogans imprinted, "RPH" and others	$65-$85
Bed Doll, 25" high, nurse uniform with "RPH" sewn on, has "V" on cap and top of apron, 1943	$425-$575
Broach, Statue of Liberty, pewter, "RPH" on banner, original card, Preview Creations	$65-$75
Calendar/Thermometer, "Our Country! Right or Wrong Our Country!", "RPH," 1943	$35-$50
Chalkware, carnival prize, baby wearing pistol belt, holster and navy cap, holding two pistols, pedestal "RPH"	$95-$120
Cigar, 14" x 1-1/4", "Pearl Harbor, Here We Come," "RPH," E.B. Stickler, York, PA, 1942	$125-$150
Drinking Straw Cover, 1-1/4" x 7", "RPH," white paper/red printing, Rainbow Straws, Jay Dee Products Co. NY, 1942	$10-$15
Flag Pole Stand/Pencil Holder, 3" x 9", RWB, "RPH," "Keep 'em Flying," All American Products Co., Chicago, 1944	$35-$50
Heel Plates (taps), "Victory," "RPH," E-Z On Co., St. Louis	$20-$25
Key Chain Tokens, 1", bakelite	$10-$15
Knife, folding, 3-1/2" x 3/4", "RPH," RWB. Made in U.S.A, 1942	$65-$85
Movie Poster, "RPH," Don "Red" Barry, Alan Curtis, Republic Studios, 1942	$450-$550
Neck Tie, child's, 36" x 3", "RPH" repeated in silver colored stitches on brown fabric	$50-$65
Painting, velvet, 30" x 16", "RPH," flag/ships in harbor	$275-$350

Item	Value
Pamphlet, recruiting, 4" x 6-1/2", paper, "Coast Guard," "RPH," "Don't Wait/Enlist Today," U.S. Government Printing Office, Jan. 21, 1942	$100-$120
Pennant, 8" x 24" triangle, "RPH" and "Let's Go Americans," Miss Liberty with "United For Victory"	$65-$85
Pennant, 8" x 24", triangle, "RPH" and "Let's Go Americans," Uncle Sam rolling up his sleeve	$75-$95
Pillow Sham, 14" x 16", "Don't Forget Pearl Harbor," "We Will Win," RWB, 1942	$55-$65
Pillow Sham, 14" x 16", "RPH," Aloha Hawaii, yellow/red/blue, 1942	$55-$65
Pillow Sham, 14" x 16", "RPH," Bowman Field, KY, purple/white, 1943	$45-$55
Pillow Sham, 14" x 16", "RPH," Fort Bragg, red/gold, 1944	$45-$55
Pin, goldtone, 2-1/2" x 2-1/2", eagle on top, pearl in center, "RPH," 1942	$300-$350
Pin, plastic, with pearl, script, original card, by Lady Patricia, blue	$75-$85
Pin Tray, milk glass, 4-1/2" x 3-1/4", "RPH"	$100-$125
Plaque, 9-1/2" round, "God Bless America," "RPH," "United We Stand"	$85-$100
Plaque, desk, 1-3/4" x 10", reverse on glass on wood stand, "RPH," "And Don't Forget Manila," gold on black	$95-$110
Plate and Cup, 9-1/4" diameter, white/blue, "RPH," U.S. Navy, U.S.S. Arizona, Seammell's Trenton NJ, 1942	$65-$95
Postcard, 3-1/2" x 5-1/2", full color, "RPH," Uncle Sam spanking Japanese child, E.C. Kropp Co.	$15-$20
Poster, 27" x 41", "We Highly Resolve…," "Remember Dec.7th!", tattered U.S. flag	$90-$120
Poster, Uncle Sam holding sailor with knife in back, B/W, 14" x 20", "RPH"	$85-$100
Ruler, 6", RWB, "RPH"	$25-$35
Sign, 19" x 26", "Vough's Grocery Store NY, V, RPH," plywood one of a kind, 1942	$300-$400
Sign, metal, fluorescent, 14" x 18", RWB, "V" shape with flag and "RPH" beneath, Pontiac Sales/Service, WI, 1942	$250-$300
Tie, 36" x 3", maroon, red/white, "RPH"	$50-$65
Vanity Case, (compact), 3" x 3", enameled lid, U.S.S. Idaho, 1943	$200-$225

Cap, 11-1/2" x 4", "RPH" on one side and "Keep 'em Flying" on the other, Capital Advertising Co. Detroit, 1943 ($75-$100).

Hand bag, 8-1/2" x 14-1/2", "RPH," rattan, Laszlo's Hawaiian symbols, Honolulu, 1943 ($150-$175).

Salt and Pepper Shaker, 2-1/2" x 2" x 2-1/2", shows Battleship Arizona sinking "RPH" one side, "U.S.S. Arizona, Lost Dec. 7, 1941" on other, H. Nov. Co. ($125-$150).

Plaque, 9-1/2" x 13-1/4", "RPH" above blue eagle perched on crossed U.S. and British flags, RWB ($150-$175).

Plaque, 5-1/2" x 7-1/2", "Lest We Forget That Historical Fateful Day December 7 1941 RPH," composition brown, silver, orange ($85-$100).

Glass, 4-3/4" tall, clear drinking glass with RWB "RPH Dec. 7, 1941," palm trees, ocean, island ($35-$50).

Punch Board, 11-1/2" x 18", multi-colored, "HULA HULA" dancing girls, sailors and palm trees, "RPH" across top ($300-$375).

Banner, 9" x 12", RWB, gold, lustrous fabric suspended from wooden dowel, "RPH" over eagle/planes/ships ($125-$150).

Banner, 8" x 12", RWB, "RPH" and "Unite for Victory," Miss Liberty holding laurel wreath, felt suspended from dowel ($100-$125).

Mechanical Pencil, RWB, "Not Forget Pearl Harbor, blue "V" ($35-$45).

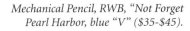

License Plate Attachments, top, from left: "RPH," RWB, "V," 4-1/2" x 4-1/2", two crossed U.S. flags, 1942 ($75-$100); "Buy U.S. Defense Bonds," 10" x 5-1/2", Erickson Mfg. Co., Des Moines, IA, 1942 ($150-$175); bottom, from left: "Taps for the Japs," "RPH," 1943 ($100-$125); tin with plastic insert, 4-1/2" x 4-1/2", "RPH," Emeloid Co. NJ, 1943 ($50-$65).

Banner, 5" x 6-1/4", "RPH," RWB, 1942 ($25-$35).

Ribbons and Patch, cloth, 2-1/4" x 5-1/4", 4" x 4-1/2", launching submarines and "RPH," "Keep 'em Flying," U.S.S. Seafox and U.S.S. Razorback, 1944 ($35-$55 each): "RPH" patch ($25-$35).

Scrapbook, 9-1/2" x 6-3/4", "RPH," battleship, wooden cover, 1945 ($50-$65).

License Plate with attachments, yellow/black, with "RPH" plate attachment and Victory tag, 14" x 6-1/4", made at Folsom Prison, CA, 1942 ($100-$125 set).

Pocket Mirror, 3-1/8" x 2-1/8", "RPH," RWB, 1944 ($25-$30).

Paper Decals, RWB ($20-$30 each).

Paper Decals, RWB, "RPH" ($15-$20 each).

Flag Boxes with Flags, Flag Products Inc. NY, from left: "Live With Your Flag," 8-1/2" x 5-1/2", RWB, 1943 ($20-$30); "Americanize Your Home," 6-1/4" x 8-1/4", 1942 ($20-$30); "RPH," 6-3/4" x 6-3/4" ($30-$40).

Advertising Mirror, 5" x 7", "RPH," "Keep 'em Flying," 1943 ($75-$95).

Scarf, 14" x 14", "RPH," sailor with signal flags ($35-$50).

Patch, cloth, 4-1/4" x 2-3/4", "RPH," RWB ($35-$45).

Window Sign, 8-1/2" x 11", "RPH," "V For Victory, Buy Defense Stamps and Bonds," Pillsbury Flour Co. ($30-$40).

Bank, metal, 3" round, drum shape, "RPH," "Do your part, Save for U.S. Defense Savings Bonds" ($45-$60).

Medallions, brass, 1" round, "RPH," eagle ($10-$15 each)

Panties, Novelty, 3", "RPH," "You Take Care of the Home Front/Don't Get Caught with Your Pants Down" ($20-$30).

Seals, 4" x 9", "RPH," in envelope ($15-$20).

Plaque, pressed wood, 3-1/2" x 3", "RPH," Syroco Wood Products, Syracuse NY ($25-$35).

Plaque, 9-1/2" round, "RPH," Uncle Sam/eagle ($85-$100).

Hanky, 13" x 13", "RPH," RWB ($20-$30).

Pennant, 23-1/2", blue felt, "Let's Go Americans," "RPH" ($75-$95).

Ruler, 6", "RPH," Shaw and Slavsky Co., 1942 ($25-$35).

Window Decal, 4-1/4" x 6", "RPH," eagle in gold, RWB ($15-$20).

Window Sticker, 2-5/8" x 3-1/4", "Remember the Destruction of Pearl Harbor, Hawaii, Sunday, Dec. 7, 1941," "Keep 'em Flying," "America/ Freedom" ($15-$20).

Window Sticker, 3-1/2" x 4-3/4", planes bombing ship, "RPH," RWB ($15-$20).

Auto License Plate Reflector, 3-1/2" round, red/white printing, "RPH" ($35-$50).

Chalkware, carnival prize, baby wearing pistol belt, holster and army cap, holding

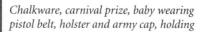

Plaque, natural wood, 8-1/4" x 3-1/2", "RPH" in black ($20-$25).

Sticker, window, 8-1/2" x 10", flag and "RPH" ($10-$15).

Newspaper Page, Sun Telegraph, Dec. 8, 1942, shows Pearl Harbor Dec. 7th ($10-$15).

Window Sticker, 9-1/4" x 7-1/4", "RPH," "We are Patriots in the Service of America," RWB ($20-$25).

Poster, 27" x 41", "We have just begun to Fight!", Pearl Harbor, soldier with M-1 rifle, list of battles ($90-$120).

Poster, 27" x 41", "Avenge December 7," angry sailor showing fist ($110-$135).

Pencil, mechanical, "RPH," Prettyman Truck Service ($40-$50).

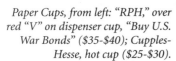

Paper Cups, from left: "RPH," over red "V" on dispenser cup, "Buy U.S. War Bonds" ($35-$40); Cupples-Hesse, hot cup ($25-$30).

Pillow, "V for Victory, RPH," eagle flying over "V," red/white ($45-$50).

License Plate Attachment, 4-3/4" x 4-1/2", "RPH" over "V" center of crossed flags, tin, RWB ($85-$100).

Pin, cello, 3-1/2", black/white, "RPH" ($35-$45).

Pencil Sharpener/Key Chain Fob, sharpener is Bakelite ($50-$65 each).

Coat Pins, "RPH," Japanese plane diving on ship, palm trees, gold/green/blue—reproduction at top ($20-$25) and original at bottom ($200-$225).

Pins, lapel, 5/8", "RPH" ($15-$20 each).

Broaches, 2" x 1", from top: "RPH," plastic goldtone ($45-$55); RWB ($35-$45).

Pins, dangle, hat from '"RPH" bar ($65-$75); flag from "RPH" bar ($25-$35).

Pins, cello ($15-$20 each).

Pins, cello, 1-3/4" ($25-$35 each).

Pins, plastic, from left: pearl, script, red ($30-$40); green ($55-$65); red/ white ($30-$40).

Pins, leather, from left: Uncle Sam holding "RPH" sign ($50-$65); fighter plane, "RPH" ($50-$65).

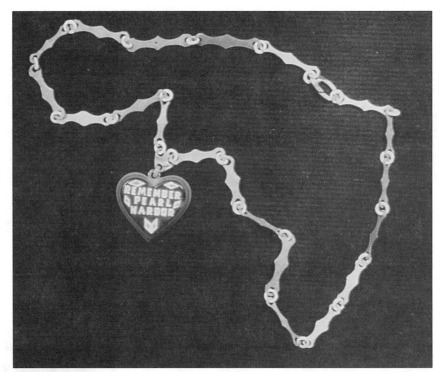

Necklace, heart-shaped, RWB, "RPH," on long linked chain ($60-$75).

Broach, anchor, rhinestones, RWB, "RPH," 1942 ($125-$150).

Pin, abalone, "RPH," 1941 ($35-$45).

Pin, copper-colored, 3" x 1/2", rifle with hanging plaque, "RPH," 1942 ($75-$95).

Chalkware Cannon, 11" x 12-1/2", sailor on gun turret, "RPH" on barrel, 1943 ($175-$200).

Pin, dagger, 3-3/4" x 1-1/4", goldtone/red/pearl, 1942 ($100-$125).

Pin, plastic, dangle, red/"Keep 'em Flying," pulling white bomb/ "RPH" ($125-$150).

Pin, cello, Japanese soldier's face as target, "Keep 'em Dying," "RPH" ($65-$75).

Pin, plastic, dangle, white plane/"RPH" on banner from red chain ($65-$85).

Pin, coat, 2-1/2", goldtone, dangle, cut out letters "Pearl Harbor" under the word "Remember" ($45-$55).

Eagle, chalkware, 5-1/2" x 7", gold/RWB, "RPH" on base ($175-$200).

Pin, lighthouse, 1-3/4" x 3-1/2", gold/RWB/pearl, "RPH," 1943 ($75-$100).

License Plate Attachment, "Taps for the Japs," 4-1/2" x 10", "RPH," Keep 'em Flying ($100-$125).

Comic Book, "RPH," 8" x 10-1/2", Street and Smith, 1942 ($45-$55).

Patch, 5" oval, "EXSO," "RPH," "V" with wings ($45-$55).

Pins, cello buttons, 1-1/4", flags, "RPH" ($20-$30 each).

Pin, goldtone plane flying toward pearl with RWB "RPH" from rear of plane ($125-$150).

Ribbon, glow in the dark, 9-1/2" x 1-3/4", red/white, "Pearl Harbor" ($25-$35).

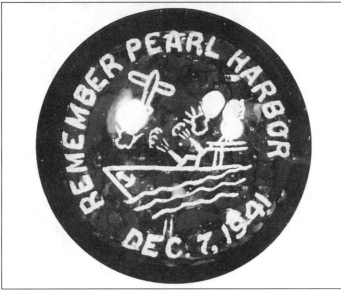

Paperweight, glass, "RPH," Dec 7, 1941, ship/plane ($55-$65).

Pins, goldtone, from top: eagle over "Remember [faux pearl] Harbor"; eagle over "RPH" ($30-$40 each).

Pins, cello/tab ($20-$30 each).

Pins, cello buttons, "RPH," RWB ($15-$20 each).

Matchbooks, "RPH" themed ($5-$10 each).

Chapter 2
Sweetheart Jewelry

Collecting sweetheart jewelry is an exciting way to preserve a unique piece of our history and great heritage of the World War II era. A gift given to a sweetheart by a serviceman strikes a deep sentimental chord in each of us. To wear a piece of patriotic jewelry was to tell the world that you cared and supported the war effort. Sweetheart jewelry included pins, lockets, wings, necklaces, pendants, earrings, bracelets and rings and was an important morale builder on the homefront.

Victory pins: Victory pins are among the most popular of the homefront collectibles. They range in size and quality, in design and accouterments from a small simple brass "V" worth about $5, to a larger "V" in sterling with rhinestones worth $65 to a few in platinum with diamonds worth well into the thousands.

This 22nd letter of the alphabet (V) became a symbol of hope not only in this country and to her allies, but also for millions of people suffering under the yoke of Nazism. To the Dutch it meant *yryjheid* (freedom), to the Czechs it meant *vitezsivi* (victory), to the Serbs is was *vitesivo* and to the French it was *victoire*.

In Morse Code, "V" is three dots and a dash, which appears with the "V" on most Victory pins. German soldiers in occupied countries were so harassed by the "V" (with its corresponding Morse Code showing up on walls and sidewalks, being tapped out on doors, being sung and whistled) that they actually began to use the symbol themselves!

Wings: "So fly with me, you mighty men/With God's aid overhead/We'll roar a million plane salute/In the land where the angels Tread." —*Lionel Croll*

A great WWII collectible is Sweetheart Wings. A large number of these fascinating pins were manufactured during the war years and are highly prized today. They came in a variety of materials, such as leather, Lucite, wood, mother-of-pearl, plastic, sterling, 10K and 14K gold and hard-cast metal. Wings often illustrate a branch of service or military specialties like an Air Force Command Pilot, Senior Pilot, Pilot, Navigator, Observer or Crew Member, or Navy Pilot, Flight Surgeon or Nurse.

Compacts: Military and patriotic compacts of World War II are fun to collect. Reasonably priced and in varying shapes and colors, they can be found looking like an

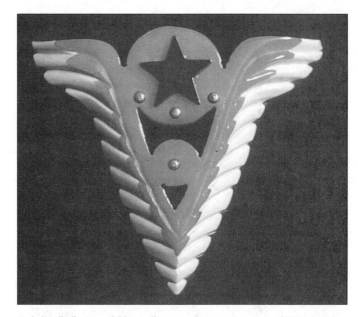

Bakelite "V" pin, red/blue/yellow, one star-son in service ($250-$325).

Army Officer cap or in an oval, heart, square or rectangular shape and displaying Uncle Sam or a comic theme. In all colors and from every branch of military service and in varying home front themes, to hunt for a unique WWII compact is always a joy.

Military rings: As homefront jewelry collectibles go, military rings tend to be a bit harder to find and higher priced. Not as many were manufactured and, as most were worn by men, they tended to experience rougher use. Ranging from 14K gold to base metal, these rings were often purchased from fine jewelers, post exchanges or they were handmade by natives or by the soldiers and sailors themselves. The most popular themes for wartime rings were military branches and specific units.

Service branch jewelry: The Army, Navy, Air Force and Marines, even the Cost Guard and Seabees had special jewelry items made just for them. Every Soldier, Sailor, Airman, and Marine had a wide variety of sweetheart items that he could buy and send to a loved one back home. Bracelets, earrings, lockets and pins were so popular and so many were produced that they are some of the best values in WWII collectibles today.

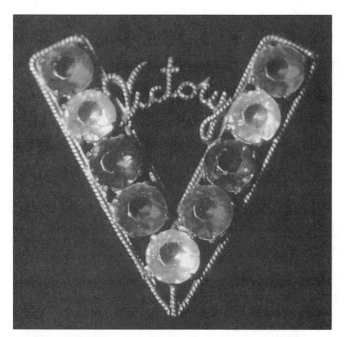

"V" pin, yellow metal, "Victory" written in wire in center of "V", large RWB artificial stones ($65-$75).

"V" pin, American Flag, "V" dangle, all in RWB beads ($65-$75).

"V" pins, including Sonja Hennie, some handmade ($45-$60 each).

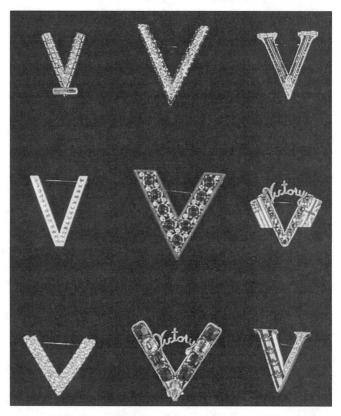

"V" pins, all with artificial stones ($50-$75 each).

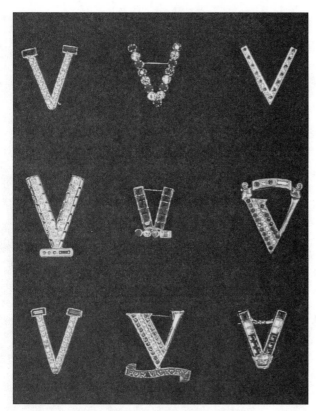

"V" pins, all with artificial stones ($50-$65 each).

Various "V" pins with plastics, metal, rhinestones and mother-of-pearl ($50-$65 each).

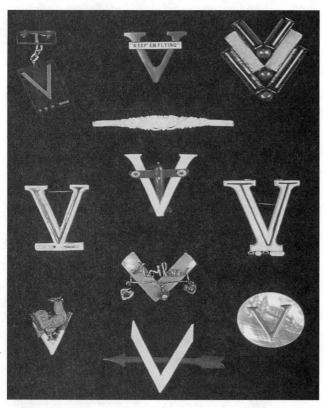

Assorted "V" pins in clear plastic, ivory and mother-of-pearl ($50-$65 each).

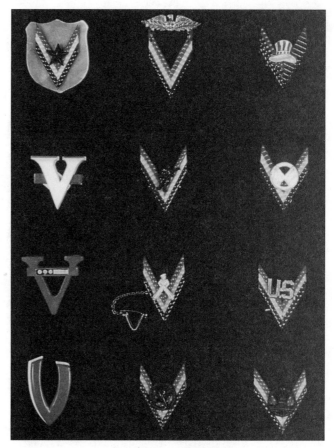

"V" pins, all in plastic or Bakelite ($50-$65 each).

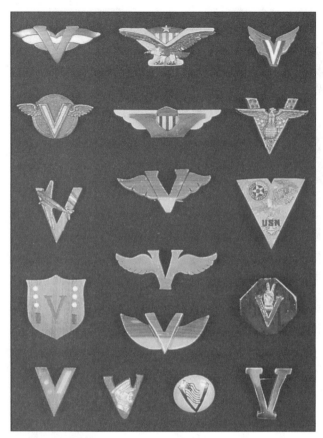

"V" pins, assorted, most of wood, coconut shell, plastic or resin ($45-$60 each).

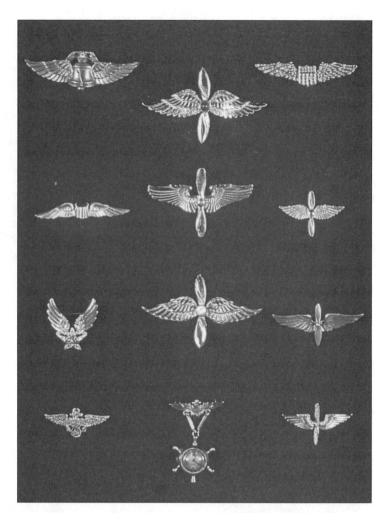

Wings, (12), assorted, navy, wing/prop ($60-$85 each); with watch dangle ($150-$165).

Pins, Plastic, Soldier, Sailor, Uncle Sam, Marine ($95-$115 each).

Compacts: on the top row are "Kamara" types, as they look like billows-type cameras ($65-$75 each).

Army-motif compacts ($75-$85 each).

Rings: top seven are hand made ($50-$65 each); bottom 10 are Air Force: top row center is mother-of-pearl ($75-$85); top row right is gold ($150-$175); second row left has gold heart ($100-$125); second row right is gold ($150-$165); others are $85-$135.

Rings: top display are Army and Air Force and bottom are Navy.; $50-$65 each except for top row #1, 4th row #1 and #4, 5th row #4 ($150-$165 each).

Wing, Air Force Senior Pilot, rhinestone 3-1/2" ($85-$100).

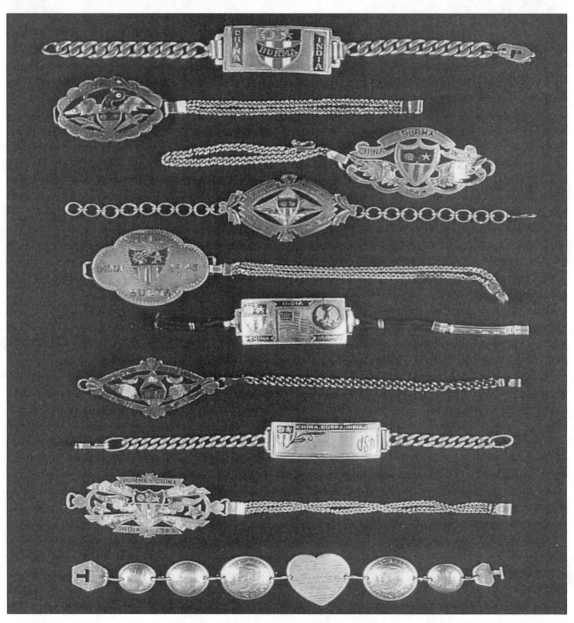

Bracelets, 9 of them are Paratrooper: top row ($200-$225); 6th row ($175-$200); 8th row ($150-$165); 10th row ($85-$100) the rest ($150-$250).

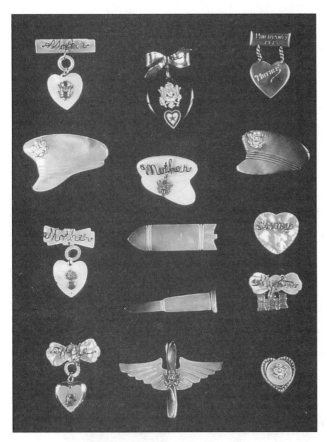

Pins, Army, mother-of-pearl ($50-$75 each).

Pins, Army, hearts: ($45-$75 each).

*Pins, Army—1st and 3rd pin on bottom row
are made from projectiles ($50-$75 each).*

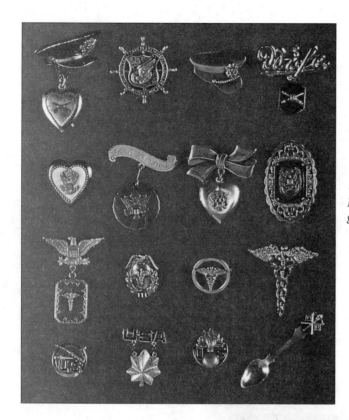

Pins, Army, shows branch of service, grade ($35-$60 each).

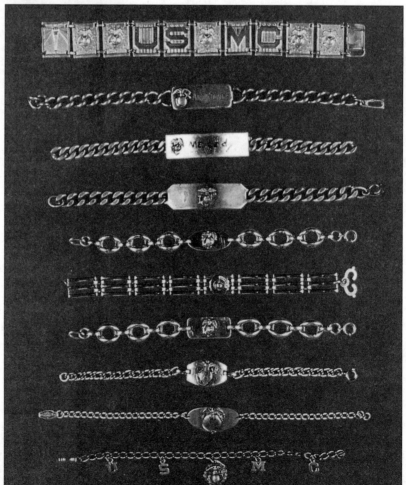

Bracelets, Marines: top is $100-$125 and the rest are $60-$75 each.

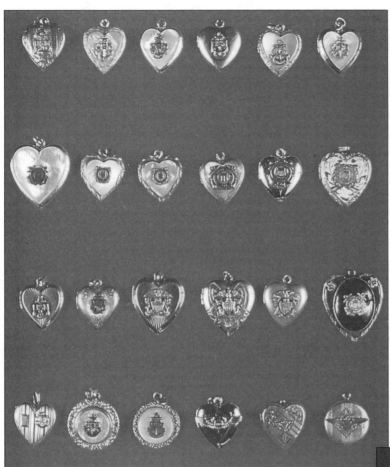

Lockets, Navy/Coast Guard ($50-$65 each).

Pins, Navy, wooden, ($35-$50 each).

Pins, Marines, hearts ($60-$85 each).

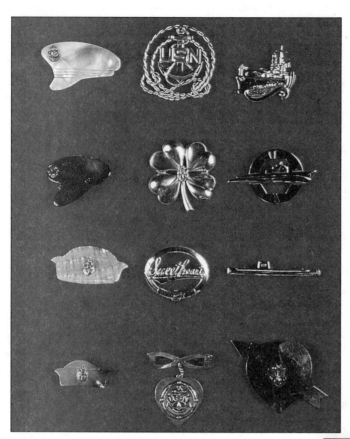

Necklace, Air Force, AF insignia on blue heart ($100-$125).

Pins, Navy: the two submarine pins are $100-$150 each and the rest are $45-$70 each.

Bracelets, Air Force: top row USAC is $100-$125; rows 2, 3, 4 are $45-$65 each; and rows 5-9 are $65-$85 each.

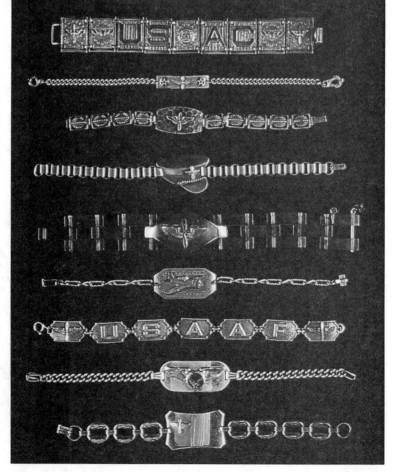

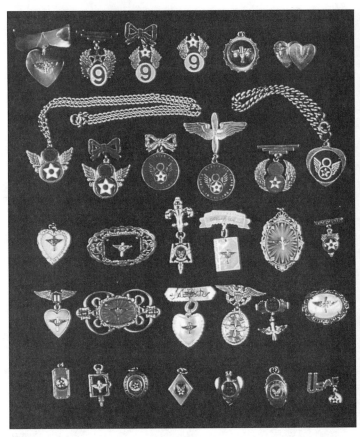

Pins/Necklaces, Air Force: rows 1-3 are $40-$65 each; row 4 are $35-$55 each; row 5 are $25-$45 each.

Pins, Air Force ($40-$75 each).

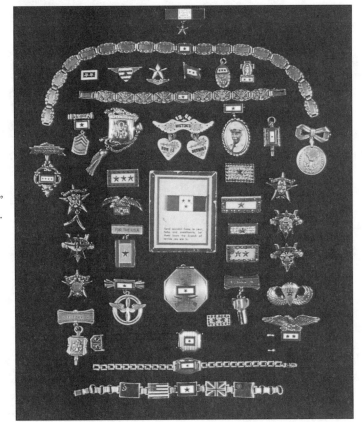

Pins, Necklace, Bracelet, "In Service" items ($40-$125 each).

Chapter 3
"V" for Victory

On Jan. 14, 1941, in a radio broadcast from London, as the story goes, it was a Belgian refugee who first urged people of all the oppressed nations to undermine the Axis morale by waving two fingers in a "V" shape indicating "V" for Allied victory. This sign quickly became World War II's most poignant and enduring symbol.

Homefront items showing the "V" sign can be discovered at military, antique, collector and vintage clothing shows and shops as well at garage sales and flea markets and now even on the Internet. These items are often found colored in the traditional red, white and blue, and can appear in any form from natural wood or cardboard to platinum. "V" sign collectibles are a major part of the vast homefront category collectors refer to as "Patriotics."

As we shuffle through the postcards, peek through the glass display cases, and scan the tables we see the numerous matchbook covers, labels, stickers, pins, hankies and pillow shams that once summoned nations to unite in the spirit of Victory. We who appreciate the devotion, and sometimes high risk, that is associated with the single letter "V" know why the WW II items carrying the "V for Victory" are so precious and collectible today.

V-Mail: Nicknamed "funny mail" because of its compact size, V-Mail became an invaluable link between our GI's and the homefront. The serviceman or woman would write only in the blank space provided on one side of the letter, then fold it so the envelope side was exposed. An Army Post Office overseas would receive the letter and an APO examiner would read it, deleting any parts the censor thought inappropriate for the family to whom it was addressed. The letter side was then photographed on 35mm film reels, then sent by air transport to the U.S. for developing at a Kodak plant and folded to 3-3/4" x 4-5/8" and delivered to the addressee. The purpose of this process was to reduce the size and weight of the mail.

Picture Frame, 10" diameter, RWB, star and "V" ($35-$45).

Item	Value
Booklet, "Victory, I'm Helping," 6-3/4" x 3-3/4", RWB, to record war bond purchases, Northwestern Mutual Fire Association	$10-$15
Booklet, "Victory Guide," 8-1/2" x 5-1/2", gray/white, for Officials of the 4-H Club, General Mills	$20-$25
Buttons, clothing, 9-count, 4-1/2" x 3", "V" shaped on card	$15-$20
Carryall, "V"...- Shopper," RWB, 35" x 15" x 12-1/2", wooden, two wheels	$250-$300
Carryall, "Victory Carryall," RWB, 29" x 14" x 8", 4 wooden wheels, "Buy War Bonds and Stamps," heavy cardboard	$175-$225
Easter Card, "From One in the Service Who Loves You," 8" x 10", RWB, large flowered "V" with gold eagle top, Gibson	$25-$35

Item	Value
Flag Stand, wooden base, 4" x 7", cardboard/paper	$35-$45
Glass Set, 9-1/2" pitcher with six 5" glasses, white eagle flying over blur "V"	$125-$150
Hankie, "V" for Victory," 12" x 12", RWB	$35-$45
Lamp, "Victory," 12-1/4" x 7", hand with fingers in "V" position, red "V" between fingers	$225-$300
Mailing Container, "V" mail, RWB, 4-1/2" x 14"	$25-$35
Padlock, brass with "V," Kingston Co.	$20-$25
Pennant, U.S. Army/Navy, 24" x 10-1/2", "V" for Victory in the Pacific	$50-$65
Pin, bakelite, red "V", dangles from blue & yellow, bar	$350-$425
Pin, celluloid, "7th Victory War Loan," 5/8" x 1", RWB, "V," "On to Tokyo," Crosley Corp	$30-$40
Pin, celluloid, "Farm Machinery," 1-1/4", RWB, "It's All In Good Repair for Maximum Production," Moline Machinery Co.	$25-$35
Pin, celluloid, "Lewis Victory Collection Contest," 1-1/4", blue over red "V," "Scrap and Salvage Campaign"	$25-$35
Pin, celluloid, "Mister Victory," 7/8", RWB, blue "V"	$25-$35
Pin, celluloid, "Production for Victory," 1-1/8", RWB, "V"	$25-$35
Pin, celluloid, "STARS & STRIPES FOREVER!," 1-1/8", RWB, "V," flag	$25-$35
Pin, celluloid, "Victory Club," 1", RWB, "V," Mutual Savings Bank of Mass	$25-$35
Pin, celluloid, "V-E Day," 1-1/4", RWB, May 8, 1945	$35-$50
Pin, celluloid, "V-J Day," 1-1/4", RWB, Aug. 15, 1945	$35-$50
Pin, celluloid, "Victory Depends on Me," 1-1/4", RWB, "V," stars/stripes,	$25-$35
Placard, "God Bless Those In Our Service, on to Victory," 5-1/2" x 6-1/2", RWB, cross in center, white stars on "V," J. Horace McFarland Co.	$25-$35
Sign, paper, 5" x 22", "Closed for V-DAY!", RWB, Butler Bros. Co.	$65-$75
Sign, neon, "We're in to Win," 4" x 12" x 5-1/2", RWB	$150-$175
Sign, "Victory Food," "Uncle Sam, Maine Potato," 4" high with large paper folder with directions, RWB	$175-$200
Stamps, assorted "V" designs, block of 6, The National Poster Stamp Society, Chicago	$20-$25
Sprayer, garden, "Bug-A-Boo," 4 oz. RWB, Socony Vacuum Oil Co.	$30-$40
Sticker, "Victory," 3-3/4" x 4-3/4", thumb up behind "V," Bentill Press, Boston. 1941	$15-$20
Sticker, "We Will Win," 8", Roosevelt looking through "V," soldier/sailor on each side, RWB	$20-$25
War Encyclopedia, "V for Victory!," 4-1/2" x 6-1/2", RWB, Harper Pub. 1942	$20-$25
Wick, "Victory," asbestos, 1/2" x 4-1/2", RWB box of 4, Atlas Asbestos Co.	$15-$20
Wrench, 1-1/2" long, "V" on handle (one of a series), box is white, Dargen, Whittington and Conner	$30-$45

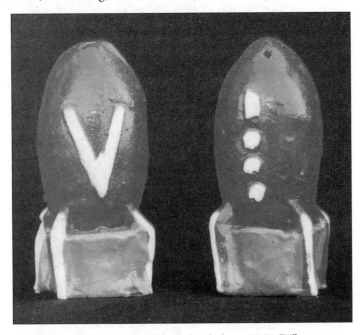

Salt and Pepper Shakers, 3-1/2" high, bomb shape, RWB, "V" on one and "…-" on other ($35-$45).

Patch, "Junior Defense Patrol" sewn on child's sweater, "V" with eagle ($65-$75).

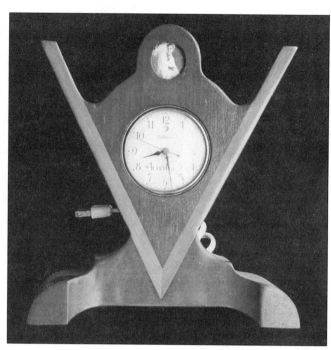

Clock, walnut with light wood "V," 10" x 11", Electric, Acushnet Co. ($100-$125).

Container, mailing for "V" mail, 4-1/2" x 14", RWB cylinder ($30-$45).

Scrapbook, "Victory," 11" x 14", "Keep a Record of America at War," flag/planes ($35-$45).

Decal, "Golden Eagle V-Gas for Victory," 3-1/2" x 4-3/4", fleshtone hand in "V" gesture ($25-$35).

Sign, glass on chain, "The "V" That Will Bring Ultimate Victory," 5-3/4" x 6-1/2", hand holding bible ($75-$100).

Display Figure, "We Can, We Will, We Must," 14" x 15", "V" behind flag, RWB ($175-$225).

Counter Display, Oxford Pocket Watches, "A Big Watch 'V' alue," 12 watches ($250-$300).

Carryall, "Victory Shopper," blue, 37-1/2" x 12" x 9-1/2", wooden, two wheels ($175-$225).

"V" mail and ink, 100 sheets, 6" x 9-3/4", RWB, Parker "Quink" Ink, paper by Charles V. Brandt Co.: paper ($20-$30); ink ($10-$15).

Chalkware, bookends, 4-1/2" x 4-1/2", Liberty Bell with "V," silver ($65-$75).

Booklet, "Victory Vacations," 8-1/2" x 5-1/2", RWB, Peck-Judah Travel Co., 1945 ($10-$15).

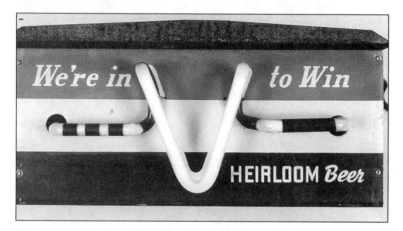

Neon "V," "Heirloom Beer," Changeable Neon Co. ($300-$400).

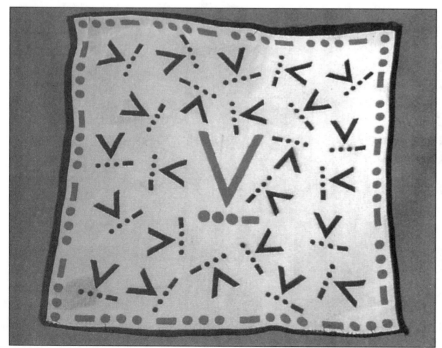

Handkerchief, 8-1/2" x 8-1/2", red "V" in center surrounded by blue "V"s, RWB ($25-$35).

License Plate Attachment, 5-1/3" x 7", tin, "Victory," shield shape, red "V," RWB ($75-$95).

Banner, "Welcome Home," 18" x 22", RWB, two U.S. flags crossed over "V," eagle flying/holding flag, cotton ($35-$50).

Chalkware, Uncle Sam standing in the center of "V," 8-1/2" x 12-1/2", RWB ($100-$125).

Fly Swatter, "Victory," 19" x 4-1/4", RWB, "Keep 'em Rolling," U.S. ($100-$125).

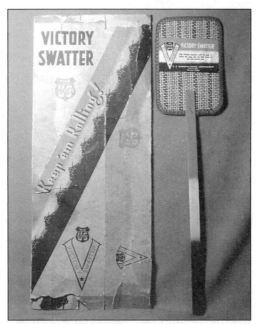

License Plate Attachment, 10" x 4-1/2", tin, red "V" behind blue "Victory" ($75-$95).

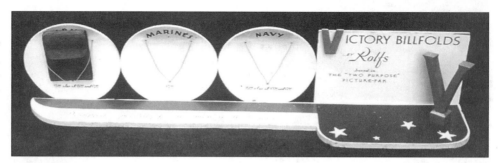

Store Display, "Victory Billfolds," 30" x 7" x 5", wood, Army, Navy and Marine billfolds, RWB, "Rolfs, The Two Purpose Picture-Pak," without billfolds ($100-$125).

Shipping Container, overseas "V," 4-1/2" x 1/2" x 8-1/2", metal, red/white ($50-$65).

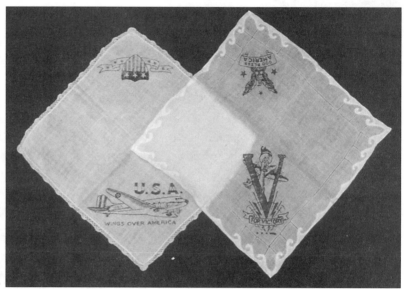

Hankies, 12" x 12", iron-on transfers, "V," wings over America ($15-$20 each).

Glasses, set of three, "Victory," RWB, 5" high ($50-$60 for set).

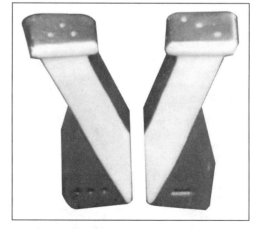

Salt and Pepper Shakers, "V" halves, 2-3/4" x 3", RWB, chalkware ($50-$65).

Apron, "Gardening for Victory," 15" x 22", cotton with front pocket ($85-$100).

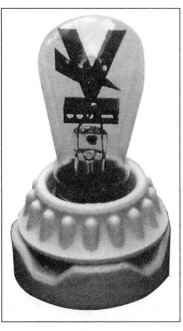

Light Bulb, "V" 3-1/2", glows purple with "…-" ($50-$65).

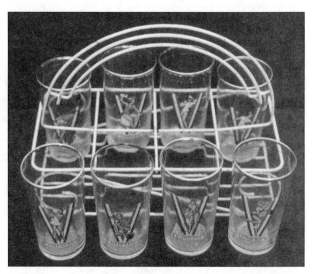

Glass Set, 8 pin-up Civil Defense drinking glasses with carrier, various uniforms on "V" RWB ($175-$200).

License Plate Attachment, 4" x 5-3/4", tin, "Victory," large red "V"/flag, blue "Victory" above ($75-$95).

Washboard, "Victory," 12-1/2" x 24", glass/ wood, "Use this washboard made of materials not needed in the war effort and help win the war," National Washboard Co. ($45-$55).

Price Board, coal, 30" x 19-1/4", Central Fuel Corporation, RWB, orange/black ($55-$65).

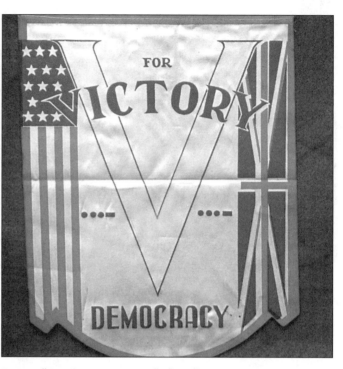

Banner, "For Victory Democracy," 9" x 12", RWB, American and British Flags, 1945 ($65-$85).

Light, fluorescent, 17" x 19", RWB with flag sticker, "United We Stand/ Divided We Fall" ($150-$175).

Flower vases, 6" x 4", white/blue/yellow, "…-" at base, Metlox Pottery, CA, 1944 ($30-$40 each).

Headband, "V" for Victory, 3" x 11", RWB ($20-$30).

Hair Pins, "Victory," 2" x 3", gray/white/black ($8-$10).

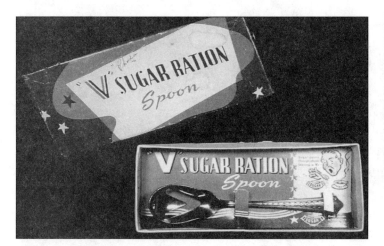

Spoon, sugar ration/cut-out "V" on cowl ($110-$135).

Napkin Set, "V" set in holder, 8-1/2" x 6", Tom Lamb ($45-$55).

Sticker, "V for Victory," 4" x 6", RWB, shield ($8-$10).

Sticker, "Our Heart is in Victory," "V" shape red heart in center, RWB ($8-$10).

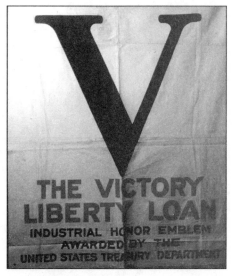

Banner, "The Victory Liberty Loan," 20" x 28", cotton, RWB ($85-$100).

Matchbooks, "V" theme ($5-$7 each).

Waxed Paper, "Victory Pack" 12" x 18", lady looking through "V" ($30-$45).

Matchbooks, "V" theme ($5-$7 each).

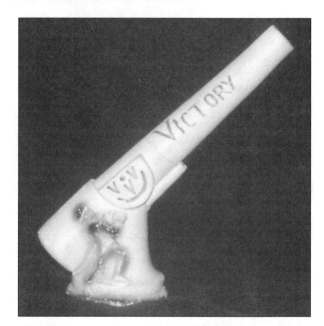

Chalkware, cannon, "Victory," 9" x 10" ($75-$95).

Pencil Lead, "Eversharp V Mail," RWB, Small Tube ($15-$20).

Slippers, baby, "Victory," straw, Philippines ($35-$50).

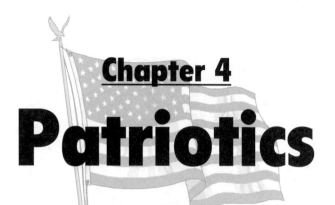

Chapter 4
Patriotics

Advertising

During World War I, Theodore Roosevelt said: "There can be no 50/50 Americanism in this country. There is room here for only 100% Americanism." This sentiment was also true for World War II. Items on the homefront that symbolized that patriotic fervor could be found everywhere in society and in countless variety.

One of the most revered symbols on the homefront that epitomized patriotism was the window banner with the red trim and blue star on white background that symbolized a family member in the service. This symbol also appeared on jewelry and can be seen on books, prints and art from the way years. While the banners with one star are more common, one can also find banner with multiple stars or with a gold star representing the ultimate sacrifice during a war.

During World War II, it was originally thought to cancel sporting evens in the United States, such as professional baseball. However, it was decided that sports could be used to lift morale in America and increase patriotic spirit. Game programs from both professional and amateur sporting events used patriotic illustrations often featuring the American flag or Uncle Sam. It was at this time that playing "The Star Spangled Banner" became the traditional opening to sporting events.

Individuals could demonstrate their support for America and the war effort by wearing pins and buttons

Sign, "Give-WAR FUND," 22" x 36", Royal Crown Cola, fiberboard ($150-$185).

with patriotic symbols and slogans. Phrases such as "Keep 'em Flying" became as well known as the Statue of Liberty. The colors red, white and blue and the American flag were used on all manner of things.

The patriotic symbols of World War II found their way into many mass-produced items. Stationery, brightly printed envelopes, postcards and greeting cards used a variety of symbols to encourage patriotism. All Americans, even children, used patriotic war stickers called "Cinderellas," to show support of the war on the homefront.

Item	Value
Chesterfield cigarette carton box, "For Christmas It's Chesterfield," 4" x 8" x 1",	$65-$75
Victory Chicken Box, rooster crowing from roof, 10" x 6" x 4", Dee Jay Farms, Loveland, OH	$75-$100
Poster, "Oakite," 11" x 14", "For the War Worker"	$25-$35
Sign, 7-Up, "Buy War Bonds," 14-1/2" x 21-1/2", elderly couple, cardboard, 1943	$75-$85

Ad, Chesterfield Cigarettes, 4" x 8", "For Mildness and Better Taste," Female Wave Officer ($25-$35).

Ad, International Harvester, 10-1/4" x 14", "Power for Victory…Power for Peace," ($4-$5).

Ad, Philco Corporation, 10-1/4" x 14", Uncle Sam handing knife to Axis leaders "Made in U.S.A." ($10-$15).

Ad, Coca-Cola, 10-1/4" x 14", "Have a Coca-Cola—You're my kind," female British officer with U.S. female Marine sergeant, 1944 ($10-$15).

Ad, Inter Woven, 10-1/4" x 14", "The greatest name in socks," Santa choking Hitler, holding Tojo and standing on Mussolini, 1944 ($10-$15).

Ad, Inter Woven, 10-1/2" x 14", "Time for some GOOD SOCKS," GI with rifle chasing Japanese soldier, 1942 ($10-$15).

Ad, Cadillac, 10-1/4" x 14", "Cannon on a rampage at 30 miles an hour!", tank firing cannon ($4-$5).

Ad, Nestle's Chocolate, 10-1/2" x 14", "Chocolate is Fighting Food," series of 10 colored action shots ($4-$5).

Ad, Seagram's 5 Crown, 10-1/2" x 14", "Lettuce Beet the Axis," Hitler being knocked out of Victory Garden ($10-$15).

Ad, Florida Grapefruit Juice, 10-1/2" x 14", "THESE are the days that call for VICTORY VITAMIN C," soldier with Thompson submachine gun in native canoe ($4-$5).

Ad, Whitman's Chocolates, 10-1/2" x 14", "A Woman Never Forgets a Man Who Remembers," AAF officer kissing a pretty woman, 1944 ($4-$5).

Ad, The WAC, 10-1/2" x 14", "Mine eyes have seen the glory…," WAC looking toward sky with shadows of soldiers ($5-$10).

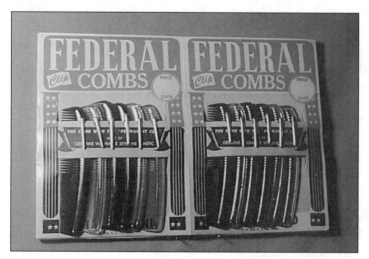

Combs, Federal, 11-1/2" x 8", double pack, 12 combs with clips on RWB display ($65-$85).

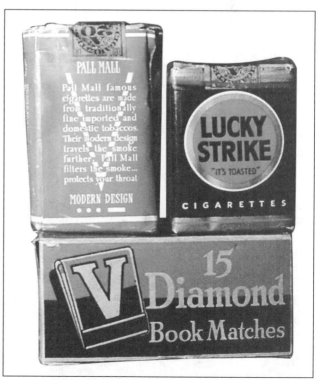

"V" Box 15 Matchbooks by Diamond ($15-$20), Cigarettes, Pall Mall "V" pack ($35-$45), Lucky Strike greens ($45-$55).

Record, Pepsi Cola, make a recording and send it home, "For Service Men and Women" ($25-$35).

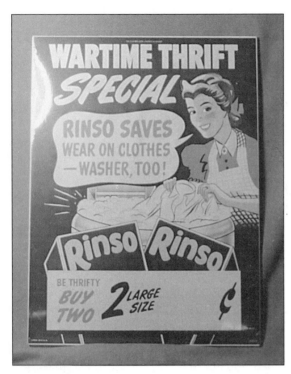

Ad, Rinso Laundry Soap, 11" x 16", "Rinso saves wear on clothes-washer too!" cartoon woman washing clothes in automatic washer ($25-$35).

Poster Coca-Cola, 15" x 13", cardboard, "B-25 Mitchell" ($65-$95).

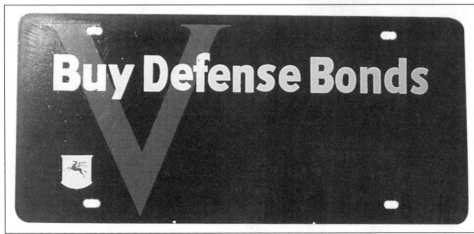

Automotive License Plate Sign, Mobil Gas, "V," "Buy Defense Bonds," RWB, fiberboard ($85-$100).

Ghiradelli Cocoa, in cardboard container, top states "Victory Pack—To Conserve Metal" ($25-$35).

Poster, "Rin-So White," 11" x 14", "Rinso Gets Out More Dirt," 1944 ($25-$35).

Cap, "Key Furniture," 11-1/2" x 4", leatherette, brown, "KEEP 'EM FLYING," Capital Advertising, MI, 1943 ($55-$65).

Calendar, Remembrance Advertising, 23" x 11", 1943 ($65-$85).

Display, Counter, "Victory Combs," 11" x 10", Vulcanizes Rubber, NY Co., 1944 ($55-$75).

Display, Counter, "Mighty Midgett Lighters," RWB, Western Insurance Co., NY, 1944 ($150-$200).

Food Can Labels, U.S. food emblems and patriotic themes ($15-$20 each).

Cigarette Carton, "Wings," Soldiers/Planes ($100-$125).

Bottle, Milk, 9-1/2" high, Uncle Sam, Maple Grove Dairy, Maple Grove, IL ($75-$85).

Bottle, Bug-A-Boo, "Victory Garden Spray," 4 oz., Socony Vacuum Oil Co. ($30-$40).

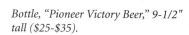

Bottle, "Pioneer Victory Beer," 9-1/2" tall ($25-$35).

Bottle, Beer, 9-1/2" tall, "Buy U.S. War Bonds," Metz Brewing Co. ($25-$35).

Bottle, Beverage, 9-1/2" high, "Victory Beverages," R. Co. ($25-$30).

Shade, Window, 36" x 7", "Air Raid Protection" ($40-$50).

Gloves, Leather, 13" x 6-1/2", tan, "Victory Welders," Women's War Workers ($55-$65).

Clocks, Alarm, 5" x 5", "War Alarm," one wind up and one electric ($45-$65 each).

Sharpener, Razor, Save for Victory; Rust Preventer, R.M. Hollingshead Corp., 1944; Replacement Soles, Treds, Auburn Rubber Co. ($15-$25 each).

Ad, Pillsbury, 6" x 7" x 8", "Pillsbury Best Flour Offers 4 Victory Star Tumblers," RWB, cardboard carrier holding 4 glasses ($85-$100).

Sign, "It's Chesterfield," 4" x 8", cardboard, Claudette Colbert, Paulette Goddard, Veronica Lake ($65-$85).

Magazine, The Red Barrel, Coca-Cola Co., January 1943 ($10-$15).

Arcade Postcards (Pin-Ups)

Arcade postcards with pin-up art, called "girlie cards" with risqué captions, were especially appealing to the imagination of our GIs at home or abroad. These colorful postcards showed a full-length view of a sexy female and were reproduced from legendary pin-up paintings by Gil Elvgren, Earl Moran, Zoe Mozert, George Petty, Alberto Vargas and others. Hundreds were produced and manufactured and distributed by the Mutoscope Reel Corporation and the Exhibit Supply Co. Many of these illustrations were also contracted for use on calendars, ink blotters, notepads and similar products.

Postcards, "TOKIO OR BUST" and "CHUTE THE WORKS," Mozert ($15-$20 each).

Item	Value
"A CLOTHES CALL," Elvgren	$15-$20
"ANCHORS AWEIGH," Moran	$15-$20
"CAUGHT IN THE DRAFT," Moran	$15-$20
"FIRST LINE OF DEFENSE," Mozert	$15-$20
"HIT THE DECK," pin-up, Mozert	$15-$20
"INCENDIARY BLONDE," pin-up, Mozert	$15-$20
"INFLATION CONTROL," Petty	$15-$20
"NAVAL MANEUVERS," Mozert	$15-$20
"KEEP 'EM FLYING," Petty	$15-$20
"OBSERVATION POST," Mozert	$15-$20
"PURSUIT TYPE," Mozert	$15-$20
"REDUCING WAIST," Mozert	$15-$20

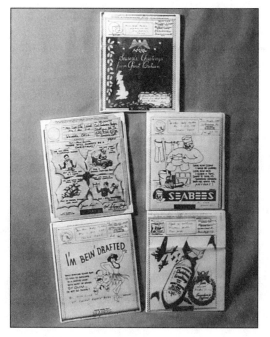

"V" Mail, cartoon covers, B/W ($20-$25 each).

Banks

Item	Value
Actual 20MM Shell, 7-1/4" x 1", "Victory Bank, Souvenir of World War II," brass with RWB label, Stoner Manufacturing Corp., Aurora, IL, 1943	$100-$125
Airplane, 5" x 12" x 9-1/2", removable cockpit "Buy a Bomber" and "Bomb Tokio," brown ceramic	$125-$150
Barrel, 2-7/8" x 2", "V" inside, "Dimes for Victory," white with brown paint, ceramic	$25-$35
Bozo the Dog, 6-1/2" x 3-1/8" x 3-1/4", "Hallow, I am the Victory Pup, Save with me for Bonds-Stamps," RWB, plaster	$100-$125
Bullet with "V," 6" x 3-1/8", brown ceramic	$65-$85
Cannon, 4-5/8" x 5" x 2-3/8", dime tube on base looks like cannon barrel, "Save for Victory Dime Bank," tin and wood, Gotham Pressed Steel Corp. N.Y.	$150-$185
Eagle on round base, 4-1/4" x 3-1/2" x 2-7/16", "Buy United States War Savings Bonds and Stamps," red, wood composition, Feibor Co., N.Y.	$50-$65
Elephant with trunk raised. 4-7/8" x 4-7/8", "V" over "…," printed in black over brown flocking	$85-$100
Elsie the Cow Cheese Box, 4-3/4" x 3-1/4" x 2", "Uncle Sam" and "Elsie says, Save for War Bonds and Stamps," wood with paper label, RWB	$85-$100
Hitler Pig, 3-1/2" x 4-3/4", Hitler painted on butt of pig, "Cents 4 Defense," "Camp Adair, Oregon" on hip, ceramic, Botay, Kansas City, MO	$200-$250
Junior Minuteman with child's face, 6" x 3-9/16" x 2-1/2", RWB, "National Defense Junior Minuteman Bank," wood composition, Nadine Wendon, 1941	$50-$65
MacAuthur Bust, 7-1/8" x 3" x 2-3/4", gold with black lettering on square base, "Save for Freedom," "Buy United States War Savings Bonds and Stamps" on base, Feibor Co., N.Y.	$85-$100
MacArthur Plaque, 7-1/16" x 11", glass bubble to hold coins in front of picture, RWB, "Save for Victory Bank," cardboard, wood and glass	$150-$185
Military Radio, 2-11/16" x 4-1/4" x 3", green base, silver top with black printed "V," white metal and lead	$85-$100
Minuteman, 9-15/16" x 3-5/8" x 3-5/8", memorial on wall "For Victory-Save to Buy United States War Bonds," RWB, printed on 4 sides, plaster	$85-$100
Pig with big ears, 2-1/2" x 4-1/2", "V" around coin slot, "Coins for Defense," has 12 stars (6 red and 6 blue on each side of coin slot), white with black print, ceramic	$100-$125
Pig with big ears, 3-1/2" x 4-1/2", 8 stars (4 on each side of coin slot), blue with red print, Botay, Kansas City, MO	$100-$125
Pig sitting on back legs, 4-9/16" x 3" x 3", "I'm Saving for Defense" white, pink, blue, green and brown print, ceramic	$35-$45
Sailor image burned into wooden box, 6-7/8" x 4" x 2", "Save For Victory," "Jacksonville, Fla." natural wood	$50-$65
"SAVE FOR VICTORY," tree branch, words are burned into wood. Paso Robles, CA	$20-$30
Suitcase, 2-3/4" x 3-3/4" x 1-1/2", blond wood with red, black, yellow print, "Pack Your Coins for Defense Bonds," "New York, Calif. Fla.," natural wood	$50-$65
Tank, 2-7/8" x 8" x 2-3/8", tank with rectangle turret in natural wood with burned in lettering, "Tanks for Dimes" on both sides.	$85-$100
Tank, 3" x 6" x 1-3/4", tank with round turret in natural wood with burned in lettering, "Save for Victory," Buffalo, N.Y.	$85-$100
Two-faced mascot, 6" x 3-1/2" x 3", white with brown print, "Jake-Jonah," ceramic and cardboard, Jonah and Jake Co. N.Y.	$85-$100
Uncle Sam, 9-3/8" x 4-5/8" x 2-3/8", "Uncle Sam Bank," gold, composition, durable Toy and Novelty Co.	$125-$150
Uncle Sam and Lincoln Memorial Plaque, 7-1/16" x 11", glass bubble to hold coins in front of picture, RWB, "Save for Victory," cardboard, wood and glass	$150-$185
V-shape on square base, 5-3/8" x 4-1/2" x 2", paper label, "Save Your Small Change and Buy More War Savings Bonds," white with RWB label, ceramic, Richard Nelson Co., 1940-44	$100-$125
Victory Envelope, 4-7/16" x 2-3/4", blue, (top) "Do Your Part," (middle) "Handi Pocket Victory Save to Buy War Bonds and Stamps, Save to Pay Your Taxes, Own a Share in America," (bottom) "The Citizens and Southern Keep America Free," paper, American Bank Service Company, WI, 1940-41	$25-$35

Desk Phone, 3-7/8" x 4-3/8" x 5-5/16", "Tele-Victory 1, Save for War Bonds and Stamps," RWB, cardboard, F.E. Company, Chicago, 1942 ($85-$100).

"V" War stamp with picture of soldier, 5-7/8" x 3-3/4" x-7/8", square penny tube, yellow and RWB, "War Stamps, You Buy 'em, I'll Fight 'em," Electric Corporation of America, 1942 ($125-$150).

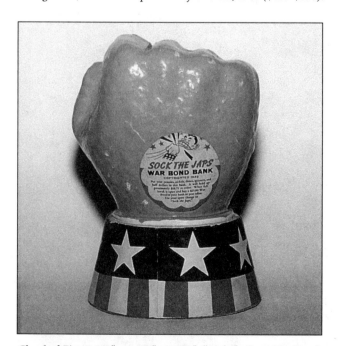

Clenched Fist, 5-5/8" x 3-7/8" x 3-1/2", "Sock the Japs, War Bond Bank," flesh tone/RWB, Styrofoam, Lite Products Corp., 1942 ($125-$150).

Mail Box, 4-9/16" x 2-1/4" x 1-7/8", green/RWB, "Save for War Bonds and Stamps," cardboard ($65-$85).

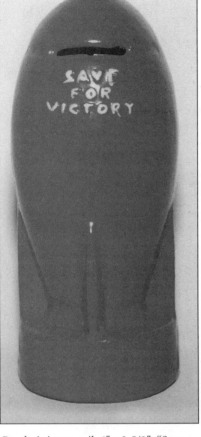

Bomb, round, screw-on top, 4-1/4" x 4-1/4", red with gold, "Savefor Victorious Day," steel ($65-$85).

Drum, 2-1/4" x 3-1/8", "Remember Pearl Harbor—Do Your Part, Save for U.S. Defense Savings Bonds," RWB, tin, Ohio Art Company ($125-$150)

Bomb sitting on tail, 6" x 2-5/8", "Save for Victory" on front with "Buy United States War Bonds and Stamps" on base, red with white print, composition, Feibor Company, N.Y. ($65-$85).

Bazooka Shell, pointed top, 5-15/16" x 2-13/16", "Save for War Bonds and Stamps," green/RWB, steel, J. Chein Company ($65-$85).

Bazooka Shell, rounded top, 4-5/8" x 2-3/8", "Save for War Bonds and Stamps," green/RWB, steel, J. Chein Company ($65-$85).

Round Box, 1-5/16" x 3-3/8", large "V" with photo of Roosevelt, "Save for Victory" green/RWB, cardboard ($65-$85).

Uncle Sam "Jr. Saving Bank and Clock," 8" x 8-1/2", red leather clock hands, bank box is tin, RWB ($150-$175).

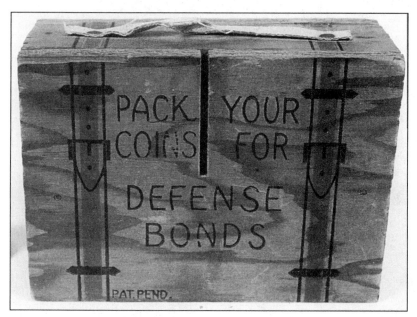

"Pack Your Coins for Defense Bonds," 1-1/2" x 3" x 3-3/4", Plywood suitcase, Cliff House, San Francisco ($25-$35).

Uncle Sam Plaque, 7-1/8" x 11", glass bubble to hold coins in front of picture, RWB, "Save for Victory Bank," cardboard, wood and glass ($150-$185).

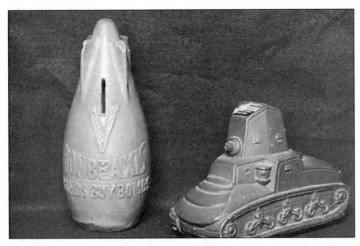

Tank, 6-1/2" x 2-3/4", O.D. green composition, coin slot on side of turret, Wellmade Doll Co. ($55-$65).

From left: Bomb, 8" x 3-1/2", "Bomb the Axis," "Buy War Bonds," chalkware, Stem-Lewis Co. Chicago, 1943 ($65-$85); Tank, 8" x 5", chalkware, "Buy War Bonds Regularly," 1943 ($85-$100).

Metal and Leatherette, 4-1/2" x 3-1/4", "SAVE FOR LIFE, LIBERTY AND THE PURSUIT OF HAPPINESS," RWB "V," Zell Prods Co., NY, 1944 ($125-$135).

"Victory Bank," 3-1/2" x 4-1/2", "Buy Bonds," silver, RWB, Eagle in "V," chalkware ($55-$65).

Drill Sergeant, 6" x 7", plaster, whistle in hand, chubby/stern face ($85-$100).

"VICTORY, HANDY POCKET BANK," cardboard, black/tan, Everett PA National Bank ($20-$25).

"BOMB BANK," 7-1/2" x 3-1/4", "Bomb the Japs from Your Home!", gray/RWB sticker, W.H. Long Co., Chicago, IL, 1942 ($65-$85).

Books (hardcover)

Item	Value
America on Guard, Thomas Penfield, Rand McNally Co., 1941	$10-$20
Battle Below, Robert Casey, Bobbs-Merrill Co., 1945	$15-$20
Defense for America, Thomas Penfield, Rand McNally, 1941	$15-$20
Front Line, J.M. Dent & Sons, 1943	$15-$20
GI Joe, Lt. Dave Breger, blue Ribbon Books, 1945	$15-$20
God is My Copilot, Robert Scott, Scribner's, 1944	$20-$25
Guadalcanal Diary, Richard Tregaskis, Random House, 1943	$20-$25
Handbook for Americans, Thomas Penfield, Libby McNeil & Libby Co., 1942	$15-$20
Here is Your War, Ernie Pyle, Henry Holt & Co., 1943	$20-$25
Hiroshima, John Hersey/Alfred A. Knopf, 1945	$20-$25
It's a Cinch Private Finch, Sgts. Ralph Stein/Harry Brown Whittlesey House, 1943	$20-$25
It's a Tough War, Collection, Garden City Publishing, 1943	$20-$25
Listen Hitler-The Gremlins Are Coming, Inez Hogan, E.P. Dutton Co., 1943	$35-$40
Low on the War, David Low, Simon & Shuster, 1941	$25-$30
Male Call, Milton Caniff, Simon & Shuster, 1945	$35-$40
Our Fighting Ships, Mitchell Katz, Herbert Lee/Edwin Levy, Harper & Bros, 1942	$15-$20
Our Navy's Striking Power, Leonard Winans, Grossett & Dunlap, 1941	$20-$25
Our Sons Will Triumph, Jack Dixon, Thomas Y. Crowell Co., 1944	$25-$30
Private Breger, Dave Breger, Rand McNally, 1942	$25-$20
Private Breger's War, Dave Breger, Random House, 1944	$15-$20
The Sad Sack, Sgt. George Baker, Simon & Shuster, 1944	$25-$30
They Were Expendable, W.L. White, Harcourt, Brace & Co., 1942	$20-$25
They're All Yours, Uncle Sam, Max Barsis, Daye, 1943	$15-$20
Thirty Seconds Over Tokyo, Capt. Ted Lawson, Random House, 1943	$20-$25
This is the Navy: The Navy in Action, Critchell Rimington, Dodd, Mead & Co., 1945	$20-$25
Up Front, Bill Mauldin, Henry Holt & Co., 1944	$25-$30
The Victory Binding of the American Woman's Cook Book Wartime Edition, Ruth Berlozheimer, Consolidated Book Publishers, Inc., 1943	$25-$30
What's New in the Air Corps, Lt. Hugh Sears, Grossett & Dunlap, 1941	$20-$25
The Wolf, Sgt. Leonard Sanson, United Publishers, 1945	$15-$20
Years of Wrath, David Low, Simon & Shuster, 1945	$25-$30

"Movies at War," Vol. II, 1943 ($20-$25).

"Lunacy Becomes Us," 5-1/4" x 13-3/4", dust cover, Hitler with wreath on head, edited by Clara Leiser, 1939 ($100-$125).

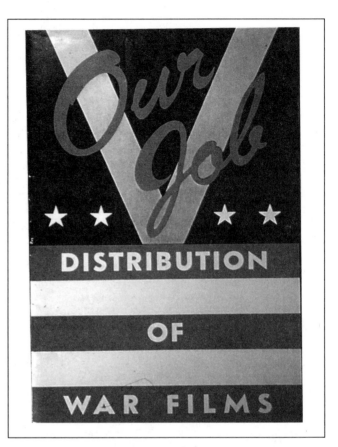

"Our Job: Distribution of War Films," War Activities Motion Picture Industry. Jan. 9, 1943 ($15-$20).

"Movies at War," Vol. 4, 1944 ($20-$25).

Books (softcover)

Item	Value
11 of the World's Great War & Spy Stories R.M. Barrows, Consolidated Book Publishers, 1944	$15-$20
Give Out-Songs of, for and by the Men in the Service, Femack Co., 1944	$20-$25
Health for Victory-ABC's of Eating for Health, Home Economics Institute, 1942	$10-$15
Meat Point Pointers, National Live Stock and Meat Board	$10-$15
More Food Through Conservation Farming-Food for Men at War, Men at Work, and Our Allies, U.S.D.A.	$10-$15
The Scrapbook of Army/Navy Humor, Industrial Tape Co., 1943	$15-$20
Servicemen's Pin-Up and Puzzle Kit, Reginald Leister, National Assoc. Service, 1943	$20-$25
USO/YMCA Hospital Kit for Convalescents, 5" x 8", 4 paperbacks: *A Road to Recovery* by Chaplain Robert Rasche, *Howl While You Heal* by Jaffe, *Think on These Things* by Everett Moore Baker and *Fun En Route*	$20-$25
Victory Meat Extenders, Plankton Packing Co.	$5-$10
Wartime Canning Booklet, Albertine Berry, Lone Star Gas Co.	$5-$10
Your Handbook, Civilian Personnel Handbook No. 8, War Dept., 1945	$10-$15

FIGHTING FORCES SERIES from Penguin Book Company

Item	Value
48 Million Tons to Eisenhower, Lt. Col. Randolph Leigh, 1945	$10-$15
Army Life, Warrant Office (JG) E.J. Kahn, 1942	$10-$15
Combat First Aid, 1944	$10-$15
The Capture of Attu, War Dept., 1944	$10-$15
Cartoons for Fighters, Sgt. Frank Brandt, 1945	$10-$15
Freedom Speaks, George F. Reynolds/Donald F. Connors, 1943	$10-$15
The German Soldier, Capt. Arthur Goodfriend, 1944	$20-$25
GI Sketch Book, Aimee Crane, 1944	$10-$15
Guadalcanal Diary, Richard Tregaskis, 1943	$10-$15
Handbook for Army Wives & Mothers, Catherine Redmond, 1944	$10-$15
A History of the War, Rudolf Modley, 1943	$10-$15
How the Jap Army Fights, Lt. Col. Paul Thompson/Lt. Col. Harold Doud/Lt. John Scofield, 1942	$20-$25
How to Abandon Ship, Phil Richards and John J. Banigan, 1943	$10-$15
How to Shoot the U.S. Army Rifle, Lt. Arthur Goodfriend, 1943	$10-$15
Island Victory, Lt. Col. S.L.A. Marshall, 1944	$10-$15
Modern Battle, Col. Paul W. Thompson, 1943	$10-$15
The Nazi State, William Ebenstein, 1944	$10-$15
New Soldier's Handbook, 1943	$10-$15
Psychology for the Fighting Man, National Research Council, 1943	$10-$15
Psychology for the Returning Serviceman, Irvin Child/Marjorie Van De Water, 1945	$10-$15
The Remaking of Italy, Pentad, 1941	$10-$15
Russia, Bernard Pares, 1944	$10-$15
The Russian Army, Walter Kerr, 1944	$10-$15
A Short History of the Army and Navy, Fletcher Pratt, 1944	$10-$15
So You're Going Overseas, Capt. Stockbridge Barker, 1944	$10-$15
Soldiers in the Philippines, William Thaddeus Sexton, 1944	$10-$15
Survival: Land, Sea, Jungle, Arctic, Airlines War Training Institute, 1944	$10-$15
The War in Outline 1939-1943, War Dept., 1944	$10-$15
They Were Expendable, W.L. White, 1942	$10-$15
Thirty Seconds Over Tokyo, Capt. Ted Lawson, 1945	$15-$20
This is the Navy, Gilbert Cant, 1945	$10-$15
Weapons for the Future, Capt. Melvin M. Johnson/Charles T. Haven, 1943	$10-$15
Why Britain is at War, Harold Nicolson, 1941	$10-$15
World War II 1939-1945, Roger W. Shugg/Maj. H.A. DeWeerd, 1945	$10-$15

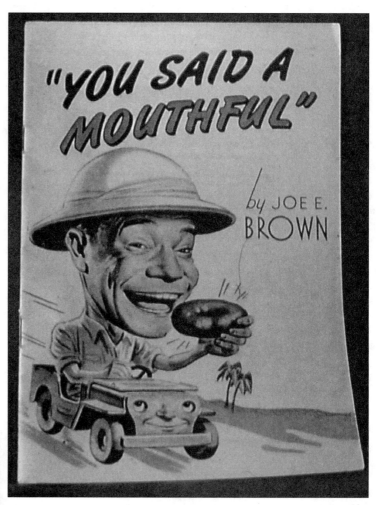

"You Said a Mouthful," Brown riding in Jeep, Joe E. Brown ($25-$35).

Booklet, "What Shall Be Done About Japan After Victory?", 5" x 7-1/4", GI holding rifle on Japanese prisoner, EM15 GI Roundtable ($15-$20).

Greeting Cards

Item	Value
"Best Wishes to a Woman in the Service," flag, flowers, 4-3/4" x 5-1/2", J.P., USA	$15-$20
"Birthday Congratulations to a Friend in the Service," puppies dressed as servicemen, 5" x 5-7/8"	$10-$15
"Christmas Greetings to a Fine Aviator," 4-3/4" x 5-3/4", pilot saluting in front of fighter plane, USA	$15-$20
"Congratulations On Winning Your Wings," P-47 and flag, red ribbon on white background, 5-3/4" x 5", Hallmark, 1943	$10-$15
"Easter Greetings to My Boyfriend in the Service," 4-3/4" x 6", flag, roses, USA	$10-$15
"Greetings and Best Wishes to a Mighty Fine Soldier," RWB, soldier in service cap, eagle over head, 4-3/4" x 5", USA	$10-$15
"Greetings," Santa taking his cap off for Uncle Sam, 4-1/4" x 5-1/4", USA	$10-$15
"Happy Birthday to You in the Service," eagle, "V," RWB, 5-1/4" x 6-1/4", USA	$10-$15
"Hey Solider, Bet 'Ya When You're Drilling, You Do Everything Just Right," solider with rifle, 5" x 5-7/8"	$10-$15
"Hi Sailor, Here's a Wish That's Too Big to Get in the Mailbox, Happy Birthday to You," dog wearing sailor cap and mailbox, 4-3/4" x 6"	$10-$15
"Hi Solider! I've Got Something Here You'll Like. Can't You Tell from My Expression," pretty young woman, 5" x 5-7/8", USA	$10-$15
"Merry Christmas Sailor, Hope Everything is Well With You," RWB, 5" x 5-7/8"	$10-$15
"Merry Christmas Solider!! Wish I could say I TOE-D YOU SO," cartoon woman writing to solider in frame, 5" x 5-7/8"	$10-$15
"Remember Pearl Harbor," Uncle Sam rolling up left sleeve, 4-3/4" x 5-3/4", USA	$20-$25
"Shoot Straight to a Happy Birthday," soldier firing a machine gun, 5" x 6", USA	$10-$15
"To a Swell Guy in the Service," cartoon of soldiers training, 5" x 5-7/8"	$10-$15
"To a Young American, Merry Christmas," Uncle Sam driving a train, 4-1/2" x 5-3/4"	$10-$15
"To My Hero on Valentine's Day," comic soldier in heart wearing campaign hat, 5-1/4" x 4-1/2", R.R.T. USA	$10-$15
"V for Victory," 4-1/2" x 4-1/2", RWB	$10-$15
"Victory Parade-Season's Greeting" (solider, sailor, nurse, marine, airman), 5" x 6", Hanover Lee Company	$10-$15

Christmas, "Hope Merry Christmas has Landed With You," 4-3/4" x 5-3/4", Marine in dress blues, flag, gifts, Storybrook Line, USA ($15-$20).

Christmas, "To a Swell Guy in the Army," 4-3/4" x 5-3/4", pretty girl looking through "V," waving flag, Storybrook Line, USA ($15-$20).

Christmas, "Ahoy There, Merry Christmas," soldier with Santa on
island, 4-1/8" x 5", Gibson, USA ($15-$20).

"A Gift for Someone in the Service from all of US," U.S. flag on padded
background, 5-3/4" x 7", Rust Craft, Boston, 1943 ($15-$20).

"A Letter to You in the Service," young girl at table with blue star
banner in background, 4-3/4" x 6" ($10-$15).

"To Someone in the Service," sailor, soldier, flyer ($5-$10).

Heroes & Stars

Item	Value
Book, Picture, *The Real FDR*, 11-1/4" x 8", Citadel Press, 1945	$10-$15
Jacket, B-10 winter, property of "Joe E. Brown," worn during USO tours, size 42, by Metro Sportswear, NY	$2,000-$2,500
Magazine, *COLLIER'S*, Admiral William F. Halsey, April 28, 1945	$10-$15
Magazine, *COLLIER'S*, General Marshall, July 24, 1943	$10-$15
Magazine, *COLLIER'S*, General Joseph Stillwell, Aug. 11, 1945	$10-$15
Magazine, *COLLIER'S*, General Omar Bradley, Sept. 15, 1945	$10-$15
Magazine, *COLLIER'S*, General Wainwright, 10-1/2" x 13-3/4", July 10, 1943	$10-$15
Magazine, General Dwight D. Eisenhower, front of flag, Curtis Pub., 1944	$15-$20
Magazine, *HOLLYWOOD*, Tyrone Power wearing flight gear from movie, "A Yank in the R.A.F.," September 1941	$75-$100
Magazine, *LIFE*, "Lt. Audie Murphy," on cover, July 16, 1945	$45-$55
Magazine, *Movie Story*, "PIN-UP GIRL REVIEW," 8-1/2" x 11", "Betty Grable," rear view in swimsuit, December 1943	$55-$75
Magazine, *Newsweek*, General Omar N. Bradley, Dec. 17, 1945	$25-$35
Magazine, *TIME*, Brig. Gen. James Doolittle, Nov. 23, 1942	$35-$45
Magazine, *TIME*, "Admiral Chester W. Nimitz" on cover, Feb. 26, 1945	$15-$20
Photo, autographed, 8" x 10", B/W, "Pappy" Boyington, U.S. Marine Corps	$100-$125
Photo, autographed, 8" x 10", B/W, 2nd Lt. Audie Murphy, U.S. Army	$450-$550
Photo, autographed, 5" x 7", B/W, General George S. Patton, dated April 16, 1944	$1,500-$1,700
Photo, autographed, 8" x 10", B/W portrait, actress/USO volunteer Carol Lombard	$900-$1,100
Photo, autographed, 8" x 10", B/W, General Omar N. Bradley, reverse, "U.S. Army Photograph," autographed: "To Major James M. Stout with highest personal regards. Omar N. Bradley"	$150-$200
Photo, autographed, Maj. Gen. Claire L. Chennault at desk, "To Cpt. William A. Cottrell, Best Wishes, L. Chennault," 8" x 10", B/W	$1,100-$1,200
Photo, autographed, "Colonel Paul Tibbits," standing near nose of "Enola Gay"	$125-$150
Photo, autographed, Pvt. Mickey Rooney, 5" x 7", Rooney and B-24 air crew in front of "Sleepy Time Gal," "Best Wishes, Mickey Rooney," 1943	$200-$225
Photos, "War Heroes Pin-Ups," 6" x 9", RWB envelope holds "Packet No. 6" set of 12 official photos of U.S. War Officer Heroes, sepia portraits, each 4" x 7" with biography (Halsey, Wainwright, Kenny, Clark, Ingersoll, Wassell, Gilmore, Bulkeley, Eaker, Swett, Scott, Whitehead), 1943	$150-$200
Photos (same as previous), "Packet No. 4" (Doolittle, Spaatz, Cannon, Kinkaid, Scott, Sherman, Morrill, Bennion, Pease, Vandergift, Wermuth, Bailey), 1943	$150-$200
Pin, Celluloid, Admiral Chester W. Nimitz, 1-1/4", RWB	$35-$45
Pin, Celluloid, Admiral William F. Halsey, 1-1/4", RWB	$35-$45
Pin, Celluloid, "Draza Mihajlovich," SLAV Hero, Leader of the Chetniks Guerrilla Army Resistance to Nazis	$35-$45
Pin, Celluloid, General Carl A. Spaatz, 1-1/4", B/W, "Tooey"	$25-$35
Pin, Celluloid, General Douglas MacArthur, RWB, "The Man of the Hour"	$45-$55
Pin, Celluloid, General Dwight D. Eisenhower, 1-1/4", RWB	$35-$45
Pin, Celluloid, General Dwight D. Eisenhower, purple ribbon, 1-1/4", RWB, "Welcome Home IKE"	$45-$55
Pin, Celluloid, General George S. Patton Jr., 1-1/4", RWB	$35-$45
Pin, Celluloid, General Jonathan M. Wainwright, 1-1/4", RWB	$35-$45
Pin, Celluloid, General De Gualle, 1-1/4", B/W	$65-$75
Pin, Celluloid, "Our Hero/Brig. Gen. James H. Doolittle," 1-1/4", B/W, April 18, 1942 Air-Raid on Tokyo.	$75-$100
Portrait, General Douglas MacArthur, 5" x 8-1/8", brownstone art of MacArthur holding binoculars, artist Carl Bohnen, 1942	$20-$25
Postcards, photo, 4" x 5-3/4", color tinted, Tarjeta Postal 1945, Van Johnson, Spencer Tracy, Betty Grable, Dana Andrews, Errol Flynn, each	$10-$15
Seal, foil, Sir Winston Churchill, 1-1/4" x 2", red and blue/silver embossed	$15-$25
Uniform, U.S. Navy, white dress cotton blouse and trousers, white sailor cap, belonging to Gene Kelly, worn in "Anchors Aweigh," MGM, 1945	$2,000-$3,000

Photo, Robert Taylor, Naval Officer, 5" x 7", facsimile autograph ($5-$10).

Magazine, LIFE, 10-1/2" x 14", Bob Hope, Jan. 10, 1944 ($25-$35).

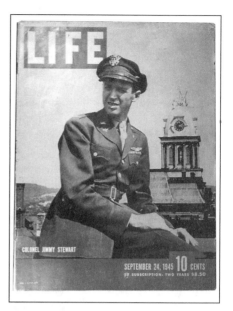

Magazine, LIFE, 10-1/2" x 14", "Colonel Jimmy Stewart," Sept. 24, 1945 ($25-$30).

Banner, "OUR HERO," Gen. MacArthur, 18" x 22", face of general ($65-$75).

Magazine, "The Life of Franklin D. Roosevelt" ($20-$30).

Magazine, LIFE, 10-1/2" x 14", "General MacArthur," Sept. 17, 1945 ($25-$35).

Chalkware, Bust, General MacArthur, 12-1/2", "V," gold-tone ($65-$85).

Magazine, LOOK, Gen. "George Patton,"
June 1, 1943 ($25-$35).

Plate, Dinner, MacArthur image with West Point
and battle scenes, B/W ($35-$45).

Poster, General MacArthur in front of flag,
11" x 14", full color ($45-$65).

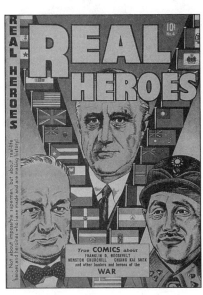

Comic Book, "Real Heroes," 7-1/2" x
10-1/4", Roosevelt, Churchill, Chiang Kai
Shek, 1942 ($35-$45).

Poster, "An Appeal from General Vandegrift:
Buy War Bonds!", 22" x 28" ($65-$85).

Print, "President F.D. Roosevelt," 11" x 14",
ships/flags ($55-$75).

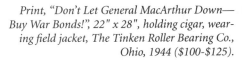

Print, "Don't Let General MacArthur Down—
Buy War Bonds!", 22" x 28", holding cigar, wear-
ing field jacket, The Tinken Roller Bearing Co.,
Ohio, 1944 ($100-$125).

Print, "Franklin Delano Roosevelt,"
8-1/2" x 11", sepia tone in printed
frame of military images ($35-$45).

Matchbooks

One of the most successful advertising tools on the homefront was the advertising matchbook. The Government and private industry distributed millions of matchbooks with color images that supported the war effort. It was "V" FOR VICTORY," "SMASH THE AXIS," "DEFEND AMERICA," "CARELESS LIPS CAN SINK SHIPS" and "KEEP 'EM FLYING." Every time a match was struck, Americans were reminded that we were at WAR and we were in it to WIN! Standard matchbook sizes are 1-3/8" x 4-3/8" and 2-7/8" x 4-3/8".

All matchbooks listed below are 1-3/8" x 4-3/8"

Item **Value**

5th WAR LOAN, Ohio Match Co...$3-$4
ALL OUT FOR VICTORY, Arrow Match Corp. ....$4-$5
BUCCANEER, Scout Bomber, Bond Bread ....$3-$4
CATALINA, Patrol Bomber, Bond Bread..$3-$4
DAUNTLESS, Diver Bomber and Scout, Bond Bread ....$3-$4
DEFEND AMERICA, Match Corp. of America..$3-$4
DEVASTATOR, Torpedo Bomber, Bond Bread......................................$3-$4
FOR PROTECTION OF OUR NATION, BUY BONDS, Match Corp. ....$3-$4
HELLDIVER, Scout Bomber, Bond Bread ....$3-$4
HI SERVICEMEN, SAN JOSE WELCOMES YOU, Ohio Match Co. ....$3-$4
KEEP DEMOCRACY FROM DYING, Match Corp. of America......................$4-$5
KEEP 'EM ROLLING, Match Corp. of America ....$4-$5
KEEP SMILING, V FOR VICTORY, Ohio Match Co. ....$4-$5
KINGFISHER, Scout and Observation, Bond Bread................................$3-$4
MARINER, Patrol Bomber, Bond Bread ....$3-$4
MILITARY INSTALLATIONS: forts, camps, fields, bases, barracks, training
    centers, shipyards and depots (Fort Ord, CA, Fort Miley, CA, Presidio,
    CA, Fort Lewis, WA, Fort Logan, CO, Fort Sumner, NM, Fort Meade,
    SD, Fort Bliss, TX, Fort Leonard Wood, MO, Fort Custer, MI,
    Fort Myers, FL, Fort Bragg, NC, Fort Miles, DE, Fort Williams, ME,
    Camp Thomas Scott, IN, Camp Shelby, MS), size is 1-3/8" x 4-3/8", each...........$3-$4
O-K AMERICA, LET'S GO!, Diamond Match Co.....................................$3-$4
PRESERVE FREEDOM NOT SLAVERY, Arrow Match Corp. ....$4-$5
PUT YOUR SAVINGS INTO WAR BONDS, Ohio Match Co. ....$3-$4
SALUTE OUR ARMY AIR BASE, SANTA ANA, CA, Diamond Match Co. ....$3-$4
SAVE WASTE FATS FOR EXPLOSIVES, Arrow Match Corp. ....$4-$5
SEAGAL, Scout and Observation, Bond Bread..$3-$4
UNITED WE STAND, National Press ....$3-$4
VINDICATOR, Scout Bomber, Bond Bread..$3-$4
WILDCAT, Fighter, Bond Bread ....$3-$4
YOU ARE WORKING TO WIN, Universal Match ....$3-$4

KEEP 'EM FLYING, Albert Pick Co. ($4-$5).

AVENGER, Torpedo Bomber, Bond Bread ($3-$4).

GENERAL MacARTHUR, Arrow Match Corp. ($8-$10).

EASY TO PICK UP VD, Universal Match ($8-$10).

CARELESS LIPS CAN SINK SHIPS, Match Corp. of America ($4-$5).

DAMN THE TORPE-DOES—FULL SPEED AHEAD, General Match ($10-$12).

REMEMBER PEARL HARBOR, General Match ($10-$15).

Miscellaneous

Item	Value
Album, "Victory Club," 7-1/2" x 10", Official Government Photographs (empty)	$15-$20
Baby Powder, Johnson's wartime container	$10-$15
Booklet, "War Birds of the U.S.A.," 7-1/4" x 7-1/8", plane identification, shows eagle flying with U.S. planes, RWB, Filen's Men's Clothing Store	$10-$15
Booklet, "Your Army," 9" x 6", Selective Service, 1942	$10-$15
Card Deck, "Army/Navy 'E' for Excellence," by Shefford Cheese Co.	$10-$15
Certificate, "U.S. Treasury War Finance Committee," 8" x 10", 22 Disney Characters, 1944	$200-$225
Cigars, "Between the Acts," Victory Package, 3" x 3-1/2"	$15-$20
"Clean up for Uncle Sam," 3" x 3-1/2", lather leaves, soapy paper, RWB, pilot	$15-$20
Clock, "WARALARM," 5" x 5", made from nonessential materials, wind-up, black/white face	$75-$100
Fan, "Buy an Interest in Your Country," 7-3/4" x 11-1/4", RWB, woman in white visor cap saluting, U.A. Colson	$40-$50
Fans, from left: "United We Stand," Gettier-Montanye Inc., (Center), "Miss Liberty," Shaw-Barton Inc., and "Pledge of Allegiance," Banker's Advertising Co., each	$40-$50
Frame, "United We Stand," "God Bless America," "Fought for Freedom, Liberty and Justice for All," 10-1/4" x 15-3/4", eagle over crossed American flags with flag of England and China, photo of Soldier in Center	$35-$50
Holder, Ration Book, Disney Characters "Super Duper Market"	$25-$30
Magazine, *Newsweek*, Marshal Kesselring, Feb. 21, 1944	$10-$15
Magazine, *Newsweek*, Nazi in Defeat, April 9, 1945	$10-$15
Magazine, *Post*, Rockwell cover, Armchair General, April 29, 1944	$15-$20
Milk Bottle, "Keep 'em Flying, Army Flyers Drink Milk," smiling pilot face	$75-$100
Milk Bottle Cap, "Keep 'em Flying," 1-3/4", RWB, wax cardboard, Raw Milk Products	$25-$35
Milk Bottle Cap, images of planes, 1-3/4", RWB, wax cardboard, Raw Milk Products	$25-$35
Milk Bottle Cap, images of submarine, 1-3/4", RWB, wax cardboard, Raw Milk Products	$25-$35
Milk Bottle Cap, images of destroyer, 1-3/4", RWB, wax cardboard, Raw Milk Products	$25-$35
Newspaper, "ATOMIC BOMBINGS!", 16-1/2" x 23", Friday, August 10, 1945, *Austin Statesman* (Texas), 1st edition, Hiroshima and Nagasaki	$45-$55
Newspaper, "JAPANESE SURRENDER IS SIGNED, V-J DAY!", 11-1/2" x 15", tabloid size Sunday, Sept. 2, 1945, *New York Sunday News*, home edition, 28 page, 1st section, news and photos of surrender	$45-$55
Newspaper, "NAZI SURRENDER, END EUROPEAN WAR!", 17" x 23-1/2", Tuesday morning, May 8, 1945, *Philadelphia Inquirer*, 28 pages, surrender articles	$45-$55
Newspaper, "PEACE," 1941-1945, *The Cleveland Press*	$45-$55
Newspaper, "WAR! OAHU BOMBED BY JAPANESE PLANES," 17" x 22-1/4", Sunday, Dec. 7, 1941, *Honolulu Star Bulletin*, 1st edition, 8 pages, photos of attack	$250-$350
Novelty, "Victory Rings," make your own rings, 1941	$25-$35
Portfolio, "WAR BOND BUDGET," 5" x 9", Norge, 1942	$5-$10
Poster, "Attention: An Industry Declared Essential," 12" x 18", paper, International Shoe Co.	$25-$30
Program, "Hollywood Victory Caravan" 9" x 12", Navy Relief Society/Army Emergency Relief, Sad Woman Holding Child Wearing Navy Cap, 1942	$50-$65
Salt and Pepper Shakers, chalkware, 2-1/4" x 3", cannons, tan	$35-$45
Scrapbook, embossed, tanks, planes, "V," 12" x 14-1/2", blue	$35-$45
Sign, "We're In It—We'll Win It!", Uncle Sam Rolling Up Sleeves, 7" x 9", double-sided, RWB, cardboard	$85-$120
Stamp Machine, U.S. Postage, "VICTORY," Uncle Sam	$200-$250
Sticker, window, 8", "We are American Citizens, God Bless America," RWB	$20-$30
Window Shade, "Air Raid Protection," 36" x 84", heavy black material on roller	$50-$65

Map, "ESSO War II," General Drafting Co. ($15-$20).

Map, "ESSO War III," General Drafting Co. ($10-$15).

Records (3), 6-3/4", Messages from Soldiers to Friends/Family," Gem Blades, USO and Salvation Army, Pepsi Cola ($35-$50 each).

Map, "Map of World Victory!", history-making dates and events, red and white, 1945 ($10-$15).

Catalog, "Decca Records Released Since 1942," 7-3/4" x 5-1/2", Decca Records, 1943 ($10-$15).

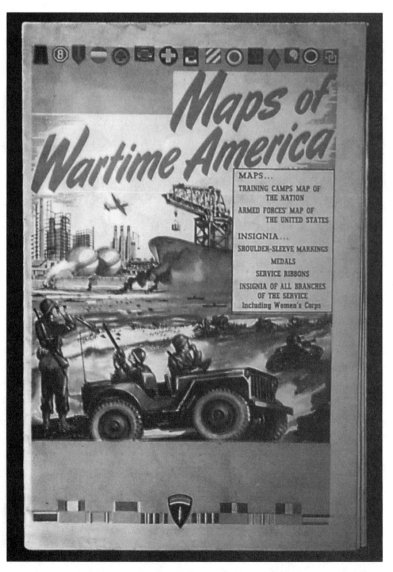

Maps, homefront (4), Global/Pacific ($15-$20).

Map, "Maps of Wartime America," C.S. Hammond ($10-$15).

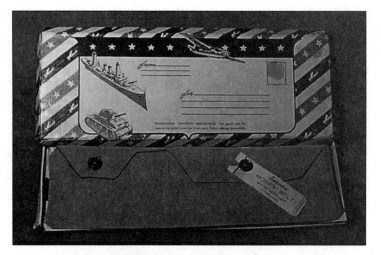

Money belt in shipping box, 9-1/2" x 4", RWB box, belt is tan ($45-$55).

Blotters (2), "Sunoco Oil," 3-1/2" x 6", "Helps Quick Starting," "Defend Your Car's Life," 1943 ($20-$25 each).

Patch, Leather, Soldier Carrying Very Large Pack, 4-1/2" x 7" ($45-$55).

Patch, Leather, "World War II," 5" x 7", Tan, RWB ($45-$55).

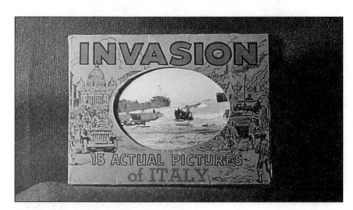

Clock, cardboard, 5-1/2" x 7-1/4", "God Bless America" Statue of Liberty, RWB, Electric, Acro Scientific Products Co. Ill. ($150-$200).

Picture Set, Invasion of Italy, 15 photos, 2" x 3-1/2", orange window package ($15-$20).

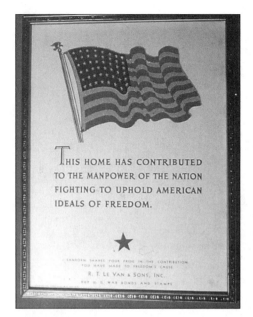

Cake Tops, wedding, 3-1/2" x 4", plaster, groom in military uniform ($35-$45 each set).

Picture, Flag Waving, 8" x 10", "This Home Has Contributed to…," L.T. Le Van and Sons, Inc. ($30-$40).

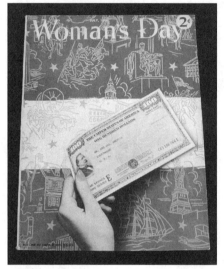

Magazine, Woman's Day, July 1944 ($15-$20).

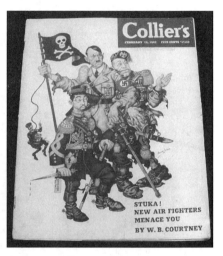

Magazine, Collier's, Feb. 14, 1942 ($35-$45).

Magazine, Collier's, soldier holding Tommy Gun on prisoners, Jan. 29, 1944 ($15-$20).

Magazine, Adventure, 7" x 9-1/4", "The End of Jingle Bill," October 1944 ($10-$15).

Magazine, What's New, published by Abbott Lab, May 1942 ($20-$25).

Magazine, Adventure, 7" x 9-1/4", "Six Weeks, South of Texas," June 1943 ($10-$15).

Magazine, Collier's, "Camp Shows," female entertainer wearing camp show uniform, July 14, 1945 ($15-$20).

Magazine, Liberty, April 24, 1943 ($10-$15).

Magazine, Liberty, July 10, 1943 ($5-$10).

Magazine, Liberty, "General George C. Kenney" on cover, Jan 15, 1944 ($5-$10).

Punch Board, "War Bond Special," 9-1/2" x 9-1/2", "All Awards Paid in Defense Stamps" ($100-$125).

Magazine, Knit For Defense, Spool Cotton Co., 1941 ($8-10).

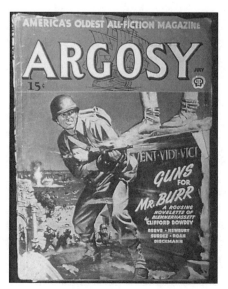

Magazine, ARGOSY, "Guns for Mr. Burr," Popular Pub., July 1943 ($15-$20).

Magazine, Post, Rockwell cover, Soldier Looking at War Bond, July 1, 1944 ($15-$20).

Photo Book, Souvenir, 9" x 12", Irving Berlin's "This is the Army, All Soldiers Show" ($15-$20).

Picture, American flag, 4-5/8" x 5-5/8", clear plastic frame, "Colors That Never Run" ($25-$35).

Calendar with thermometer, 5-3/4" x 8-1/2", Branches of Service in Corners, Female Drum Major with Flag, 1943 ($35-$45).

Postcard, American flag, 5-3/4" x 7-3/4", wooden, RWB, "God Bless America," "I'm Proud to be An American," Patriotic Art Co., Venice, CA ($25-$35).

Candy Holders, tank and ship, 4" x 1-3/4", clear glass, original candy inside, each ($35-$50).

Calendar with thermometer, 5" x 7", flag, B-17, U.S. Capitol, gold-tone frame, 1943 ($30-$45).

Bag, paper, 6" x 10", "For Gunpowder, Save Waste Fats," ($15-$20).

Booklet, "AMERICA IN WORLD WAR II," Educational printing House, Ohio ($5-$10).

Pamphlet, "Current Events," American Education, September 1943 ($5-$7).

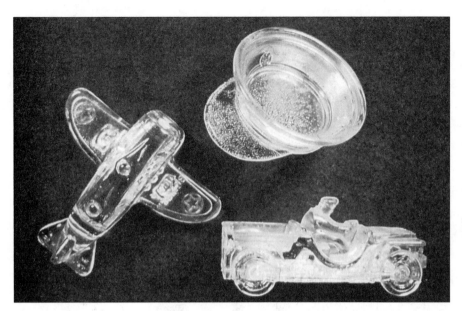

Candy Holders, plane, hat and jeep, 4" x 2", clear glass, empty, each ($30-$40).

Novelty, Miniature Panties, "Keep Out Restricted Area," "Keep 'em Flying," Camp Wolters ($25-$35).

Banner, "United States Air Force in the South Pacific," 11" x 25-1/2", 5th Air Force/U.S. Flag/ British Flag, planes bombing island ($95-$120).

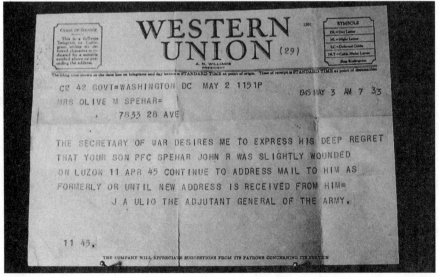

Telegram, Western Union, May 2, 1945, advising that son was slightly wounded on LUZON ($50-$75).

Sign, "GIVE: Community and War Chest," 9"
x 12", Uncle Sam pointing, RWB, cardboard
($50-$65).

Pen Holder, three soldiers in jeep, wood-
tone, Syoco Co. ($35-$50).

Sign, "WE BUY USED FAT," 15" x 18-1/2",
RWB, cardboard ($25-$35).

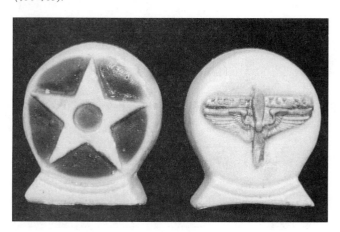

Salt and Pepper Shakers, chalkware, "Keep 'em Flying," Air Corps
emblem, RWB ($35-$45).

Towel Dispenser, "Help win the war, don't waster paper, one towel is
enough" ($150-$200).

Picture, sailor/nurse/soldier walking, 9" x 12", Harold Anderson, A.
Goes Pub., 1942 ($25-$35).

Print, nurse holding up two fingers
in "V" sign in front of waving flag,
9" x 12", C. Moss Co., 1942
($40-$60).

Movie Posters

Item	Value
Action in the North Atlantic, 27" x 41", Humphrey Bogart, Raymond Massey, U.S. War Dept., 1943	$300-$400
Air Force, 28" x 22", John Garfield, Gig Young, Warner Bros., 1943	$200-$300
Armored Attack, 14" x 22", Anne Baxter, Farely Granger, Goldwyn, 1943	$75-$100
Arms and the Woman, 14" x 22", Edward G. Robinson, Ruth Warrick, Columbia, 1944	$100-$150
At Dawn We Die, 14" x 36", Jon Clements, Hugh Sinclair, British, 1942	$100-$150
Back to Bataan, 41" x 81" (3 sheets), John Wayne, Anthony Quinn, RKP, 1945	$700-$800
Bombardier, 27" x 41", Pat O'Brien, Randolph Scott, RKO, 1943	$300-$400
Buck Privates," 28" x 22", Bud Abbott, Lou Costello, Universal, 1941	$300-$400
Captains of the Clouds, 27" x 41", James Cagney, Dennis Morgan, U.S. War Dept., 1942	$300-$400
Casablanca, 41" x 81" (3 sheets), Humphrey Bogart, Ingrid Bergman, U.S. War Dept., 1942	$1,250-$1,500
Caught in the Draft, 14" x 22", Bob Hope, Dorothy Lamour, Paramount, 1941	$100-$200
Convoy, 27" x 41", Clive Brook, Edward Chapman, British, 1941	$75-$100
Crash Dive, 14" x 36", Tyrone Power, Dana Andrews, 20th Century Fox, 1943	$300-$400
Cross of Lorraine, 14" x 11", Gene Kelly, Jean-Pierre Aumont, MGM, 1944	$50-$75
The Day Will Dawn, 27" x 41", Ralph Richardson, Deborah Kerr, British, 1942	$50-$75
Days of Glory, 27" x 41", Gregory Peck, Tamara Toumanova, RKO, 1944	$75-$100
Desperate Journey, 28" x 22", Errol Flynn, Ronald Regan, U.S. War Dept., 1942	$300-$400
Destination Tokyo, 27" x 41", Cary Grant, John Garfield, U.S. War Dept., 1943	$300-$400
Destroyer, 14" x 36", Edward G. Robinson, Glenn Ford, Columbia, 1943	$150-$200
Dive Bomber 27" x 41", Errol Flynn, Fred MacMurray, U.S. War Dept., 1941	$300-$400
Eagle Squadron, 14" x 36", Robert Stack, Diana Barrymore, Universal, 1942	$75-$100
Flying Fortress, 27" x 41", Richard Green, Carla Lahmann, British, 1942	$150-$200
Flying Tigers, 27" x 41", John Wayne, Anna Lee, Republic, 1942	$850-$950
For Whom the Bell Tolls, 41" x 81", Gary Cooper, Ingrid Bergman, Paramount, 1943	$900-$1,000
The Fighting Seabees, 27" x 41", John Wayne, Dennis O'Keefe, Republic, 1944	$550-$650
Forty Eight Hours, 28" x 22", Leslie Banks, Elizabeth Allen, British, 1942	$75-$100
God Is My Co-Pilot, 27" x 41", Dennis Morgan, Dane Clark, U.S. War Dept., 1945	$200-$300
Guadal Canal Dairy, 27" x 41", 20th Century Fox, 1943	$550-$650
Gung Ho!, 27" x 41", Randolph Scott, Alan Curtis, Universal, 1943	$300-$400
A Guy Named Joe, 14" x 36", Spencer Tracy, Irene Dunne, MGM, 1944	$250-$350
Hitler's Children, 28" x 22", Bonita Granville, Tim Holt, RKO, 1943	$150-$200
Hostages, 14" x 11", Luise Rainer, Paul Lukas, Paramount, 1943	$50-$75
I Wanted Wings, 28" x 22", Ray Milland, William Holden, Paramount, 1941	$150-$200
The Immortal Sergeant, 27" x 41", Henry Fonda, Maureen O'Hara, 20th Century Fox, 1943	$300-$400
In Which We Serve, 14" x 36", Noel Coward, Bernard Miles, British, 1942	$100-$150
International Squadron, 28" x 22", Ronald Regan, Julie Bishop, U.S. War Dept., 1941	$250-$300
Keep 'em Flying, 14" x 36", Bud Abbott, Lou Costello, Universal, 1941	$200-$300
Ladies Courageous, 14" x 36", Loretta Young, Geraldine Fitzgerald, Universal, 1944	$75-$100
Lifeboat, 27" x 41", Tallilah Bankhead, John Hodiak, 20th Century Fox, 1944	$300-$400
Memphis Belle, 27" x 41", 8th Air Force, 1944	$600-$700
Mrs. Miniver, 27" x 41", Greer Garson, Walter Pigeon, MGM, 1942	$500-$600
Northern Pursuit, 27" x 41", Errol Flynn, Helmut Dantine, U.S. War Dept., 1943	$250-$350
Objective Burma, 27" x 41", Errol Flynn, William Prince, James Brown, U.S. War Dept., 1944	$250-$350
One of Our Aircraft Is Missing, 28" x 22", Godfrey Tearle, Eric Portman, British, 1941	$150-$200
Paris Underground, 14" x 36", Constance Bennett, Gracie Fields, United Artists, 1945	$50-$75
Passage to Marseilles, 27" x 41", Humphrey Bogart, Peter Lorre, U.S. War Dept., 1944	$400-$600
Secret Mission, 14" x 22", Hugh Williams, James Mason, British, 1942	$75-$100
See Here, Private Hargrove, 28" x 22", Robert Walker, Donna Reed, MGM, 1944	$100-$150
Sergeant York, 27" x 41", Gary Cooper, Walter Brennan, U.S. War Dept., 1941	$400-$600

Item	Value
The Seventh Cross, 14" x 36", Spencer Tracy, Signe Hasso, MGM, 1944	$250-$350
Ships and Wings, 27" x 41", John Clements, Leslie banks, British, 1941	$100-$150
Since You Went Away, 27" x 41", Claudette Colbert, Joseph Cotton, Selznick Studios, 1944	$600-$800
Spitfire, 28" x 22", Leslie Howard, David Niven, British, 1942	$150-$200
Stand By for Action, 14" x 22", Robert Taylor, Brian Donlavy, MGM, 1943	$250-$350
The Story of GI Joe, 27" x 41", Burgess Meredith, Robert Mitchum, United Artists, 1945	$350-$400
Suicide Squadron, 14" x 36", Anton Walbrook, Sally Gray, British, 1941	$75-$100
The Sullivans, 28" x 22", Thomas Mitchell, Selena Royle, 20th Century Fox, 1944	$150-$200
They Died With Their Boots On, 27" x 41", Errol Flynn, Olivia de Havilland, U.S. War Dept., 1941	$350-$450
They Were Expendable, 27" x 41", Robert Montgomery, John Wayne, MGM, 1945	$550-$650
This Above All, 27" x 41", Tyrone Power, Joan Fontaine, 20th Century Fox, 1942	$350-$450
Thunderbirds, 14" x 36", Preston Foster, Gene Tierney, 20th Century Fox, 1942	$75-$100
To The Shores of Tripoli, 28" x 22", John Payne, Randolph Scott, 20th Century Fox, 1942	$200-$300
Victory Through Air Power, 27" x 41", directed by H.C. Potter, animated/live action, documentary, Disney, 1943	$400-$450
Watch on the Rhine, 14" x 11", Paul Lukes, Bette Davis, Warner Bros, 1943	$100-$150
White Cliffs of Dover, 27" x 41", Irene Dunne, Alan Marshall, MGM, 1944	$650-$750
Why We Fight," 28" x 22, directed by Frank Capra (series of 7 documentaries), 1942-1945	$300-$400
The Wife Takes a Flyer, 14" x 36", Constance Bennett, Franchot Tone, Columbia, 1942	$75-$100
Wing and a Prayer, 27" x 41", 20th Century Fox, 1944	$400-$600
Wings of the Eagle, 14" x 36", Dennis Morgan, Ann Sheridan, U.S. War Dept.	$100-$150
Yank in the RAF, 27" x 41", Tyrone Power, Betty Grable, 20th Century Fox, 1942	$900-$1,000

Winged Victory, 27" x 41", 20th Century Fox, 1944 ($100-$125).

The Bugle Sounds, 27" x 41", MGM, 1941 ($150-$200).

Pilot #5, 27" x 41", MGM, 1943 ($100-$125).

When Johnny Comes Marching Home, 27" x 41", Universal, 1942 ($75-$100).

Prelude to War, 28" x 24", narrated by Walter Houston, U.S. Army Signal Corps, 1942 ($400-$700).

Wings and the Woman, 27" x 41", RKO, 1942 ($150-$200).

The Purple Heart, 27" x 41", 20th Century Fox, 1944 ($150-$200).

Chesterfield Carton, Cardboard,
4" x 8" x 1", $65-$75

Poster, Oaklite, 11" x 14", $25-$35

Sheet Music,
Der Fuehrer's Face, 1942, $35-$45

Ad, Victory Chicken box, cardboard, 10" x 6" x 4", $75-$100

Milk Bottle, glass, "Keep 'Em Flying," 10-1/2" high, $65-$75

Patriotics

Jersey, Baseball flannel, 1943, $1,000-$1,200

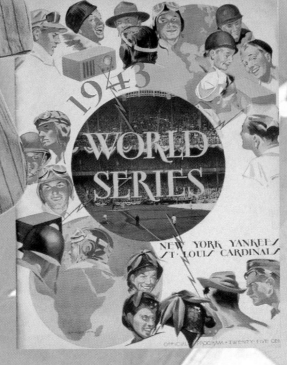

Program,
1943 World Series,
$150-$200

Greeting Card,
Christmas Greetings,
4-3/4" x 5-3/4", $10-$15

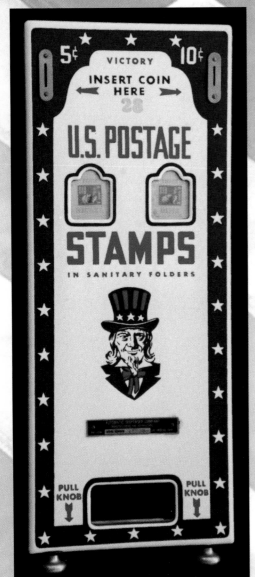

Postcards, assorted, Navy theme, 3-1/2" x 5-1/2", $6-$8

Stamp Machine, Uncle Sam, 1942, $200-$225

Magazine, *Hollywood*,
Tyrone Power on cover, 1941
$75-$100

Magazine,
General Dwight D. Eisenhower, 1943, $15-$20

Ration Book Holder,
Disney characters, 1943,
$45-$55

Patriotic Fans, $25-$35 each

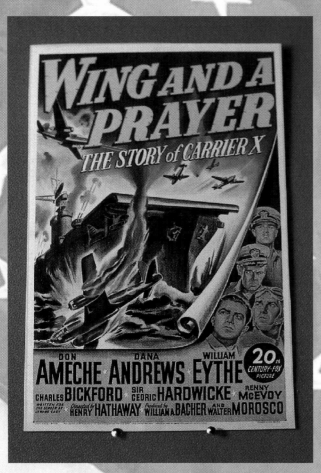

A Wing and a Prayer, 27" x 41", 1944, $400-$600

Guadalcanal Diary, 27" x 41", 1943, $550-$650

Poster, Memphis Belle, 27" x 41", 1944, $600-$700

Poster, Next, 22" x 28", 1944, $125-$165

Poster, Back the Attack, 10" x 14", 1943, $50-$60

Poster, Keep him Flying, 20" x 28", 1944, $175-$200

Poster, To Have and to Hold,
20" x 28", 1944, $175-$225

Hat made from pennant felt, $65-$85

Bed Doll, 25" high, 1943, $425-$575

Pin, gold plated with rhinestones, 2-1/2", $300-$350

Knife, folding, 3/4" x 3-1/2", $65-$85

Pillow Cover, 14" x 16", 1942, $55-$65

Assorted Pins, 1942-1943, $65-$85

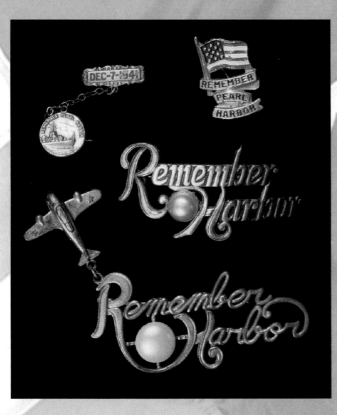

Calendar/Thermometer, 1943, $35-$50

Painting, velvet, 16" x 30", $275-$300

Poster, 27" x 41", 1942, $90-$120

...we here highly resolve that these dead shall not have died in vain...

REMEMBER DEC. 7th!

Chalk Plaque, with "V", 9-1/2" round, $85-$100

Bakelite "V" pin, red/blue/yellow, dangles from bar, $350-$425

Glass Set, 9-1/2" pitcher, 5" glasses, $125-$150

"V" for Victory

Carryall, on wheels, 29" x 14" x 8", $175-$225

VICTORY CARRYALL

Buy WAR BONDS AND STAMPS

Hankie, silk, 12" x 12", $35-$45

Flag Stand, wood base, 4" x 7", $35-$45

Stamps, block of 6, National Poster Society, $20-$25

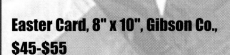

Easter Card, 8" x 10", Gibson Co., $45-$55

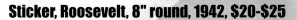

Sticker, Roosevelt, 8" round, 1942, $20-$25

Lamp, 7" x 12-1/4", 1942, $225-$300

Pin, cello button, Anti-Axis, Goldtone, $35-$40

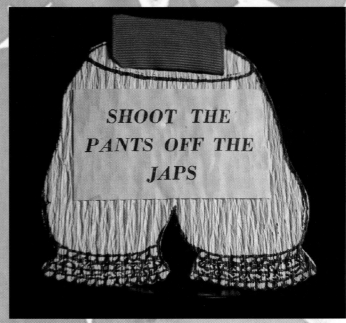

Panties, paper, Anti-Axis, 2-1/2" x 3-1/2", $25-$35

Ashtrays, glass, Hitler, Tojo, Mussolini, $195 (set)

Pin/Booklet, cello, Hitler, 1-1/2", $30-$45

Postcard, Hitler, Tojo, Mussolini,
3-1/2" x 5-1/2", $5-$10

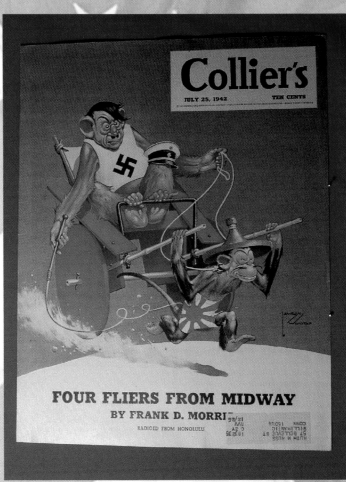

Magazine, *Collier's*, July 25, 1942, $45-$55

Bookmark, Japanese
soldier, 2-1/2" x 7", $25-$35

Display Board, Hitler, Mussolini, Stalin
22-1/4" x 22-1/4", $175-$225

Figures, Chalkware,
Tojo, Mussolini, Hitler, $750-$1,000

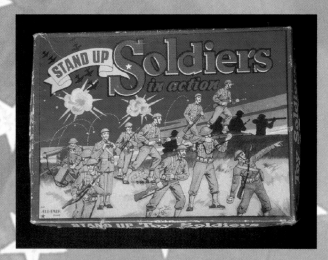

Game, Stand Up Soldiers, 7-1/4" x 10", 1944, $45-$55

Puzzles, Victory Series, 8" x 11", $30-$40

Punchboard, You're in the Army Now,
9-1/2" x 8-1/2", $85-$100

Game, Bild-A-Set, 10-1/2" x 14", 1943, $125-$150

Ukulele, Victory, 6-3/4" x 21", $1,000-$1,200

Target Game, Bomber Ball, 1942, $150-$185

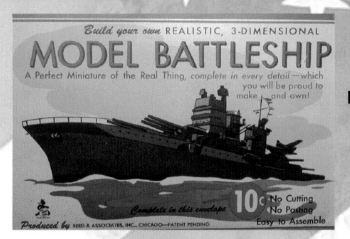

Model, Model Battleship, 7" x 9", $15-$20

Plane, Blow-A-Plane, 10-1/2" x 10-1/2", $30-$40

Victory Paintbook, $25-$30

Coloring Book, Spot Planes,
10" x 13-1/2", Merrill, $60-$75

Paper Dolls, Army Nurse, Merrill, $125-$150

Victory Playing Cards, $65-$75

Target Game, Smash the Axis, 1943, $100-$125

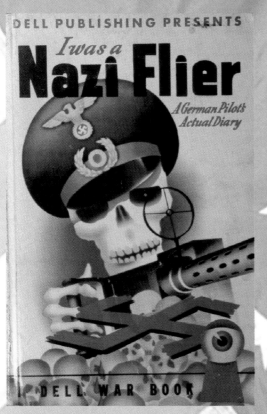

Comic Book, I Was a Nazi Flier,
Dell, 1941, $40-$50

Comic Book, Captain Midnight's
Secret Squadron, 1942, $150-$200

Comic Book,
Captain Marvel Jr., #11,
1942, $75-$85

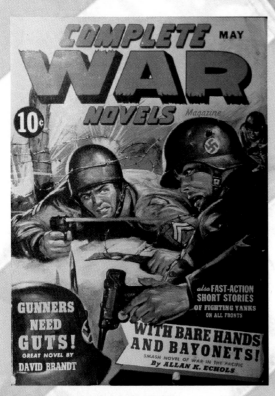

Comic Book, Complete War
Novels, May 1943, $15-$25

Comic Book, Superman, #34, 1945, $625-$750

Victory Seed Packs, by Richfield, 1944, $10-$15

Guide To U.S. Warships, 1943, $10-$15

Spotter's Dial, Target Tokyo, 1944, $20-$25

Civil Defense Equipment, armband ($25-$35), helmet ($65-$75), carrying case ($55-$65), pamphlets ($10-$15)

The True Glory, 27" x 41", Columbia, 1945 ($75-$100).

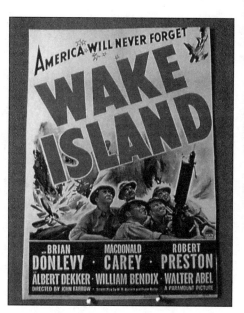

Wake Island, 27" x 41", Paramount, 1942 ($650-$750).

So Proudly We Hail, 27" x 41", Claudette Colbert, Paulette Goddard, Paramount, 1943 ($600-$800).

Thirty Seconds Over Tokyo, 27" x 41", MGM, 1944 ($650-$750).

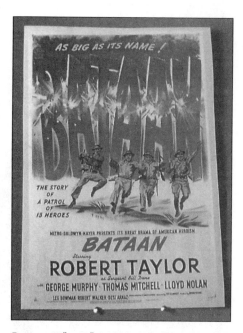

Bataan, 27" x 41", MGM, 1943 ($150-$200).

Sahara, 27" x 41", Columbia, 1945 ($600-$800).

We Are the Marines, 27" x 41", D. Louis de Rouchemont, 20th Century Fox, 1943 ($200-$400).

Attack! The Battle for New Britain, 27" x 41", U.S. Signal Corps, RKO, 1944 ($200-$400).

With the Marines at Tarawa, 27" x 41", U.S. Marine Documentary, Universal, 1944 ($200-$400).

Desert Victory, 27" x 41", British Army/RAF Documentary, 20th Century Fox, 1944 ($200-$400).

Combat America, 27" x 41", Maj. Clark Gable, U.S. Air Force Documentary, 1944 ($400-$700).

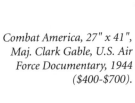

Pins

Item	Value
Pin, Celluloid, "5th WAR LOAN DRIVE: FIGHT BY HIS SIDE," Kearney & Trecker Corp., 1-3/4" dia, RWB	$25-$35
Pin, Celluloid, "6th WAR LOAN" RWB	$5-$7
Pin, Celluloid, "AGRICULTURAL VOLUNTEER WAR SERVICE 1942", 1-1/4" dia, "V" over State of Wisconsin, RWB	$15-$20
Pin, Celluloid, "ALONE AND UNAFRAID BRITISH WAR RELIEF ASSOC. OF SO. CALIFORNIA," 1" dia, British Bulldog standing on a British Flag	$10-$20
Pin, Celluloid, "BONDS FOR VICTORY CLUB: MISSOURI PACIFIC LINES, 1" dia, RWB	$10-$20
Pin, Celluloid, "BOWLER'S VICTORY LEGION 1944 V 1945, MILWAUKEE I GAVE," 1-1/4" dia, B/W	$20-$30
Pin, Celluloid, "BUY WAR STAMPS & BONDS AT RKO," 1-1/4" dia, RWB, image of Minuteman	$25-$35
Pin, Celluloid, "I BOUGHT—DID YOU?", 6th Extra Bonds, 1-1/2" dia, RWB	$15-$25
Pin, Celluloid, "JAP HUNTING LICENSE-OPEN SEASON NO LIMIT," 1" dia, RWB, crossed sword, rifle	$40-$50
Pin, Celluloid, "KILL THE RATS," 1-1/4" dia, 3 rat faces of Axis leaders (Mussi, Adolph and Togo—should have be spelled Tojo), red lettering on white background, black rats	$45-$55
Pin, Celluloid, "U.S. TREASURY BOND SELLER VOLUNTEER, THE MIGHTY 7th WAR LOAN," 1-3/8" dia, raising flag on Iwo Jima, 7th War Loan	$35-$45
Pin, Celluloid, "UNITED WAR WORK CAMPAIGN: INDUSTRY IS PLEDGED TO HELP THE BOYS," 1-7/8" dia, white center with stars and stripes shield, blue border	$15-$25

Red Cross

Pin, Celluloid, AMERICAN NATIONAL RED CROSS/NURSE PIN, brass with rim leaf design centered by RWB enameled Red Cross symbol	$15-$25
Pin, Celluloid, "AMERICAN RED CROSS BLOOD DONOR," 7/8", silver on brass, Red Cross shield, "Pro Patria"	$15-$25
Pin, Celluloid, "AMERICAN RED CROSS VOLUNTEER," enameled, 3/4", white rimmed in red and gold	$15-$25
Pin, Celluloid, "ARC WORLD WAR II," 3/4", enameled, Red Cross symbol	$20-$25
Pin, Celluloid, "NURSE INSTRUCTOR," 2-3/4", "Services of the Armed Forces," RWB	$35-$50
Ribbon, "RED CROSS SERVICE RIBBON," red and silver stripes with Red Cross symbol, pin has 9 stripes of silver (one for every 500 hours of service)	$25-$50

Other

Pin, Celluloid, "ARMY MORALE SHOW," 1-1/4", R/B, "STAFF," FT. DIX	$25-$35
Pin, Celluloid, "DORIE MILLER," 1-1/4", B/W, image of Pearl Harbor hero, Nov. 24, 1943	$50-$65
Pin, Celluloid, "I'VE ENLISTED," 3/4", RWB	$15-$20
Pin, Celluloid, "KEEP 'EM FLYING," 1-1/4", blue aircraft, white and red	$25-$35
Pin, Celluloid, "MINNEAPOLIS AQUATENNIAL," 1-1/4", RWB, soldier, sailor, marine	$15-$25
Pin, Celluloid, "REGISTERED FOR NATIONAL DEFENSE," 3/4", B/W, Iowa State Seal	$10-$15
Pin, Celluloid, "SAY IT WITH FLYERS," 1-1/4", RWB, aircraft with "V"	$25-$35
Pin, Celluloid, "UNITED AND SERVE," 1", RWB	$10-$15
Pin, Celluloid, "WWII BOND BUYER EMPLOYEE" 7/8", RWB red Stars, "Payroll Allotment Plan of Saco-Lowell Shops"	$10-$15
Pin, Celluloid, "WELCOME HOME: DISABLED AMERICAN VETERANS," 1-1/4", B/W	$20-$30
Pin, Celluloid, "WELCOME HOME OUR BOYS," 1-1/4", soldier, sailor, marine	$25-$35
Pin, Celluloid, "WELCOME HOME VETERANS," 1-1/4", B/W, Oct. 26-27, Columbia, PA	$20-$30
Pin, Celluloid, "WELCOME TO ST. LOUIS USO," 1-1/4", RWB, for United Service Organization, "Friendship and Hospitality"	$25-$35

Postal Covers

From 1941 until the end of WWII, more than 2,000 different patriotic envelopes with wartime illustrations and slogans were designed and produced. These ever popular, and often beautiful or very funny envelopes, were used to spread the message of homefront support to our servicemen and women and to each other. They were normally 3-1/2" x 6-3/8" and up to 3-1/2" x 9-1/2", and manufactured by the companies of W.G. Crosby, L.W. Staehle, Dorothy Knapp, Fluegal, Minkus and others.

Postal Covers, Envelope Cachets, 3-1/2" x 6-3/8"

Item	Value
1944 A Merry Christmas Greeting and a Happy New Year Too/This War is not Over Yet so See it Through, green, Santa Claus and Reindeer, G.H.A, 1944	$15-$20
America is not Free Until They are Freed, RWB, black, Uncle Sam and newspaper, Wake Island Marines Held by Jap Prison Camps, 1942	$20-$25
America Needs Your Help, multicolor, Minkus, 1942	$10-$15
Back and Bring Back Our Boys 6th War Loan, black, 1944	$10-$15
Between You and Me and the Lamppost the Enemy is Listening, black, FAH, 1943	$10-$15
The Big Push is on: For Victory Buy War Bonds, red and black, tanks and planes, 1943	$10-$15
Blood Donors Needed, red and black, fallen soldier, 1944	$10-$15
Bonds Built Them, green ship, 1944	$10-$15
Both Doing Their Part, black, soldier/civilian, 1945	$10-$15
Buy War Bonds A Salute to the Naval Air Force, RWB, 1944	$10-$15
Captain Colin P. Kelly, multicolor, flags and image of Kelly, 1942	$20-$25
Correct Time: Any Time to Write to G.I. Jane G.I. Joe, RWB, D. Davis, 1944	$15-$20
D-Day, Envelope, June 6th, 1944, Hitler fretting over the English Channel	$25-$35
Dear Mom, Today I bagged a Jap plane with your kitchen fats, black, women reading letter and star banner in window, 1943	$20-$25
Defender of Liberty, RWB, soldier and Liberty Bell, 1942	$10-$15
Do Your Share for Freedom and Victory Will be Ours, multicolor, torch and large V, Minkus, 1942	$10-$15
Don't Spread Rumors, red/black, House of Rumors Closed for Duration, 1944	$10-$15
E Plurbus Unum, red and black, U.S. Capitol, Minkus, 1942	$10-$15
First Day Win the War Stamp July 4, 1942, black, 1942	$10-$15
For God Prince of Peace for Country, multi flags (Jesus, globe, soldiers, sailors) Bohemian Benedictine Order, IL, 1942	$15-$20
Four Freedoms, RWB, globe and torch, V, prayer hands, 1942	$25-$30
Franklin D. Roosevelt, memorial cover (birth, death date), black, 1945	$25-$30
Full Speed Ahead Victory, multicolor, soldier image, Minkus, 1942	$10-$15
Give Generously Join, red, Red Cross, 1945	$10-$15
Give Them the Tools to Finish the Job, multicolor, Minkus, 1942	$10-$15
His V for Victory, RWB, Uncle Sam and V slingshot, 1945	$10-$15
Hoot Mon Save Everything, red and black, leprechaun with poem, 1944	$10-$15
I Have not yet Begun to Fight, multicolor, J.P. Jones, Minkus, 1942	$10-$15
I'm Working with Uncle Sam, multicolor, Minkus, 1942	$10-$15
In the Ring Until We Win, RWB, hat in ring, 1945	$10-$15
Keep That Light Burning, multicolor, Minkus, 1942	$10-$15
Let Freedom Ring for all the World, multicolor, Globe/Liberty Bell, Minkus, 1942	$10-$15
Let 'em Have It, red and black, soldier and gun, 1944	$10-$15
Let This Be America's Answer, RWB, planes in V to Tokio, 1942	$10-$15
Let's Keep it Land of the Free, multicolor, Minkus, 1942	$10-$15
Let's Put Our Hands to the Plow Protect America, multicolor, Minkus, 1942	$10-$15
Let's Work for Victory, multicolor, people and banner, 1944	$10-$15
Liberty Above All For All, multicolor, Statue of Liberty, factories and tanks, V, Minkus, 1942	$10-$15

Item	Value
Liberty We Fight for Freedom, RWB, Statue of Liberty, 1942	$10-$15
Life Liberty and the Pursuit of Happiness, RWB, Minkus, 1942	$10-$15
MacArthur of the Philippines, multicolor, banner and MacArthur, 1942	$30-$35
Memory Monday in Honor of Our Gold Star Heroes, black, B 107, 1945	$15-$20
The More at Work the Sooner We Win, black, WAT, 1945	$10-$15
On to Victory, gold and black, 1944	$10-$15
Our Country's Defenders: The United States Army, Lexington, Bataan, RWB, soldier, 1942	$15-$20
Our Heroes Awards, black, Purple Heart, 1945	$15-$20
Our Marines Can Make the Grade in Spite of Hell and High Water, black, soldiers in Ruhr Valley, Andrews Mfg., 1943	$10-$15
Plowshares Turned into Swords, green, Our Fighter Planes Rip Nazi Aerial and Ground Forces in France, Penta Arts, 1943	$15-$20
Plowshares Turned into Swords, red, Light Armed Units Mop up Jap Units in the Solomons, Penta Arts, 1945	$15-$20
Pour it on the Axis with your Waste Fat, RWB, women and two flags, 1944	$10-$15
Put Your Cash on the Line and Get the Nazi on the Rhine Buy Bonds, black, Carpenter, 1945	$20-$25
Revolutionary Men with Rifles, drum and flags (no words), 1943	$10-$15
Sacrifice with a Grin and Help the Allies Reach Berlin, red and black, man smiling, 1944	$10-$15
Then and Now Sailing for Victory, multicolor, Ships, Minkus, 1942	$10-$15
Today More Than Ever, multicolor, Lincoln, Minkus, 1942	$10-$15
Tokie Here We Come, RWB, black, emblem and ship, 1944	$15-$20
United for Freedom and Equality, multicolor, Minkus, 1942	$10-$15
United for Victory, blue, torch and people, Minkus, 1942	$10-$15
United in Defense of Freedom, multicolor, globe, Minkus, 1942	$10-$15
V on to Victory for Liberty, multicolor, planes and Statue of Liberty, Minkus, 1942	$10-$15
Victory in 1945, Yes if you do your part and conserve coal and gas, red, 1945	$10-$15
War Cover Associates, red and black, Roman soldier, 1945	$10-$15
Waste Fats Make Ammunition, green and tan shell, SS-1-B, 1944	$10-$15
We Fight for four Freedoms Freedom of Speech, black, man and child, 1944	$10-$15
We Will Win, red and black, Eagle, 1943	$10-$15
Where There is Life There is a Will to Win, multicolor, flag/plane, 1944	$10-$15
Without Freedom Liberty Dies, multicolor, Minkus, 1942	$10-$15
Work-Fight to Give Them a Better World, RWB, Uncle Sam and kids, 1942	$10-$15

Envelopes, (9) patriotic cartoon ($10-$20 each).

Envelopes, (9) patriotic cartoon ($10-$20 each).

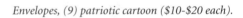

Envelopes, (9) patriotic cartoon ($10-$20 each).

Envelopes, (9) patriotic cartoon ($10-$20 each).

Postcards

Item	Value
Air Raid and Blackout, color, linen, MWM	$5-$10
All Set, color, linen, Hitler Skunk and G.I., Art One Beals	$10-$15
An Anti-Aircraft Gun Shoots Away a Ton of Copper Every 20 Minutes!, photo, color	$5-$10
The Army Put Weight on Me…and not Around the Waist!, Colourpicture Publication	$5-$10
Axis Leaders, but Mussolini has a red "X" over face, ONE DOWN, TWO to GO	$10-$15
Boeing B-17 Flying Fortress, color photo, linen, T. Art Colortone	$5-$10
Bundles for Hirohito, color, linen, MWM	$10-$15
But Sir, It Save Ammunition, color, linen, Curt Teich Army Series	$10-$15
Defend Your Country V, color, linen, Tichnor Bros., 1941	$5-$10
Dollars for Bonds Means Weapons to Win/Make Every Payday a Bond Day, B/W photo, Graycraft Card Co.	$5-$10
Due to the Gas Shortage, We Must Use Other Methods, linen	$5-$10
Gas Rationing Can't Stop Me When I'm on Maneuvers, linen	$5-$10
Ha Ha Back to the Good Old Horse and Buggy Days, color, linen	$5-$10
Haven't We Got Any Color You Like/Yes-s Officer I Haven't any Gas, color, linen, MWM General Comic	$5-$10
Hi Yo All, We're in the Army Now, color, linen, Colourpicture Publication	$5-$10
Hurrah a Letter! Now Watch Me Slap Those Japs, color, linen, Curt Teich Army Series	$10-$15
I'm All Out for Victory, screened, Benjamin Wertheimer. 1942	$5-$10
I'm Going to Wipe Them Out, color, linen, MWM Army Comic Series	$10-$15
I'm Your Air Raid Warden Lady: Put Out Your Lights and Cooperate, linen, Asheville Post Card Co.	$5-$10
Joe's Wife Bakes a Cake the Hard Way, linen	$5-$10
Join the Army and See the Sun Come Up!, linen, Metropolitan	$5-$10
Join the WAC Now!	$10-$15
Keep 'em Flying, color, linen, Longshaw Card Co.,	$5-$10
Keep 'em Flying, Dive Bomber, color, linen, Curt Teich	$5-$10
Keep 'em Flying, Fighter Plane, Curt Teich	$5-$10
Keep 'em Flying, Flying Fortress, color, linen, Curt Teich	$5-$10
Keep 'em Flying, Vindicator, color, linen, Curt Teich	$5-$10
The Last Round Up, color artwork	$15-$20
Let's Go Forward Together, color, linen, Tichnor Bros. 1941	$5-$10
Navy theme, each	$4-$8
O' Boy, Did I get Even with that Mug, color, linen, Hitler on Chamber Pot, Tichnor Bros.	$10-$15
Over the Top for Victory, color, linen, Tichnor Bros., 1941	$5-$10
PRR USO Stations Card , To Make Servicemen Comfortable, photos, multi-color, PA	$5-$10
Remember Pearl Harbor, color, linen, E.C. Kropp	$5-$10
Remember Pearl Harbor, We'll Get 'em in the End, plus 18 other postcards in fold out pack. color, linen, E.C. Kropp Co.	$25-$30
Setting the Rising Sun, color, linen, E.C. Kropp Co.	$10-$15
Silly to Waste Ten Tires on One Truck, So I Turned Six Back to the Government, color, linen, Private Berger series by Graycraft	$5-$10
So We'll Meet Again/Buy More War Bonds, color, U.S. Treasury Dept.,	$5-$10
Strive for Victory, color, linen, Tichnor Bros., 1941	$5-$10
These Supply Trains Will Continue Moving as Long as You Folks Buy Bonds, B/W photo, U.S. Army	$5-$10
United States Army "V" Postcard, R/B screened, distributed free at Army camps	$5-$10
V theme, each	$5-$10
Victory is Our Goal, color, linen, Tichnor Bros., 1941	$5-$10
Wanted: Big Reward Offered/I'm Coming Home Rich, Axis Leaders, color, linen, MWM	$10-$15
We'll Get 'em in the End, color, linen, E.C. Kropp Co.	$10-$15
Weather Reports: Hot in the Lower Regions Following a Heavy Reign, color, linen, E.C. Kropp Co.	$10-$15
What We Found in Last Night's Blackout, color, linen, MWM	$5-$10
The Yanks are Coming: Watch the Little Yellow Man Yell-O, color, linen	$10-$15

Large Letter Postcards

3-1/2" x 5-1/2", (multicolored), linen, "Greetings From" Military Bases, Fields, Camps, Forts, Barracks and Training Centers, made by Curt-Teich & Co., Chicago ($4-$8 each).

BAER FIELD AIR BASE, IN, 1941
BIGGS FIELD, TX, 1942
CAMP BEALE, CA, 1943
CAMP BLANDING, FL, 1942
CAMP CAMPBELL, KY, 1943
CAMP CARSON, CO, 1942
CAMP COOKE, CA, 1942
CAMP CROFT, SC, 1941
CAMP DAVIS, NC, 1941
CAMP GRANT, IL, 1941
CAMP HAAN, CA, 1943
CAMP HALE, CO, 1943
CAMP HOOD, TX, 1943
CAMP HOWZE, TX, 1943
CAMP LeJEUNE, NC, 1942
CAMP McCOY, WI, 1942
CAMP MAXEY, TX, 1943
CAMP PENDLETON, CA, 1942
CAMP PERRY, OH, 1943
CAMP RUCKER, AL, 1942
CAMP SHELBY, MS, 1942
CAMP WOLTERS, TX, 1942
CAMP YOUNG, CA, 1943
CHANUTE AIR FORCE BASE, 1941
FARRAGUT NAVAL CENTER, 1943
FORT BENNING, GA, 1942
FORT BLISS, TX, 1943

FORT BRAGG, NC, 1941
FORT CAMPBELL, KY, 1941
FORT CUSTER, MI, 1941
FORT GEO WRIGHT, WA, 1943
FORT JACKSON, SC, 1941
FORT KNOX, KY, 1944
FORT LEONARD WOOD, MS, 1941
FORT MEADE, MD, 1943
FORT MYERS, FL, 1943
FORT ORD, CA, 1942
FORT RILEY, KS, 1941
FORT SHERIDAN, IL, 1942
GEIGER FIELD, WA, 1943
GREAT LAKES TRAINING CENTER, chrome, 1945
HAMMER FIELD, CA, 1943
LOWRY FIELD, CO, 1942
MARCH FIELD, CA, 1942
MAXWELL FIELD, AL, 1941
MOODY FIELD, GA, 1942
PARRIS ISLAND, SC, 1942
RANDOLPH FIELD, TX, 1942
SMOKY HILL FIELD, KA, 1942
SPENCE FIELD, GA, 1942
TYNDALL FIELD, FL, 1942
WILL ROGERS FIELD, OK, 1942
WILLIAMS FIELD, AZ, 1943

Air Force-theme postcards ($5-$10 each).

"Tonight I leaned across 10,000 miles and kissed you!", helmeted soldier kissing beautiful woman in clouds ($10-$15).

Victory ($4-$8).

Various Army, large-letter postcards ($4-$8 each).

"The Captain says: Young man, you're not taking the Navy seriously!" ($10-$15).

Linen postcards ($5-$10 each).

Posters

Item	Value
Back the Attack, 10" x 14", 3rd War Loan, Schreiber, 1943	$50-$65
DIVIDE and CONQUER, 22" x 28", black and white, Hitler with noose whispering to man, U.S. Government Washington, D.C.,1942	$100-$125
Keep 'Em flying, BUY WAR BONDS, 20" x 28", pilot entering cockpit, U.S. Printing Office	$175-$200
NEXT!, 22" x 28", helmeted soldier looking down onto Island of Japan, 6th War Loan, 1944	$125-$165
Of the troops and for the troops: MILITARY POLICE, 27" x 41", combat MP signaling to stop holding whistle	$225-$275
This Year Give a Share in America, 22" x 28", smiling Santa Claus, DEFENSE Bonds and Stamps	$75-$95
To Have and to Hold!, WAR BONDS, 20" x 28", helmeted soldier holding waving flag, U.S. Treasury Dept., 1944	$175-$225

Make Haste Safely, U.S. Army Safety Program, national eagle with red shield ($25-$35).

VOLUNTEER FOR VICTORY, 11" x 14", Offer your Services to your American Red Cross, female in blue uniform and cape ($65-$85).

Bring Him Home Sooner, 22" x 28", Army sergeant waving at gate, BUY WAR BONDS, Abbott Laboratories ($125-$165).

Spars, 27" x 41", female enlisted Coast Guard sailor with field glasses, 1944 ($250-$300).

*RIGHT BEHIND HIM, 20" x 28", soldier
with rifle in front of train ($65-$75).*

*Bigger 7th War Loan, 27" x 41", people
lined up with money in hand, U.S. Treasury
($95-$125).*

*LET'S ALL FIGHT, BUY WAR BONDS, 22" x 28",
soldier attacking with rifle and bayonet, U.S. Printing Office, 1942 ($125-$150).*

*He's SURE to Get V Mail, 22" x 28", soldier
holding letter, Schlaijker, 1943 ($100-$125).*

*We Can't Win Without Teamwork, etc....,
20" x 27", soldiers looking through range
finder, R. Miller, 1944 ($75-$100).*

*Keep 'em Flying, 20" x 30", soldier and face of
Uncle Sam, C.C. Beall, 1941 ($125-$150).*

You buy 'em we'll fly 'em!, 20" x 28", U.S. Treasury Dept., 1942 ($200-$250).

They're fighting harder than ever, Are YOU buying MORE WAR BONDS than Ever?, 20" x 28", by Hewitt, charging soldiers with tank in background and yelling helmeted soldier in foreground, U.S. Treasury Dept., 1943 ($175-$225).

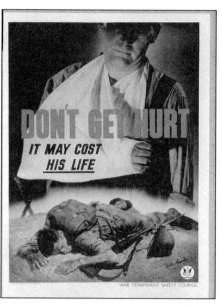

DON'T GET HURT it may cost his life, man with arm in sling over dead soldier, 22" x 28", U.S. Dept. Safety Council ($125-$150).

The Nazis Burned These Books, but free Americans Can Still Read Them 22" x 28" ($125-$150).

Let's Finish the Job! EXPERIENCED SEAMAN NEEDED, 22" x 28", sailor at helm ($125-$150).

HELP BRING THEM BACK TO YOU, Make Yours a Victory Home!, 22" x 28" ($85-$100).

POW-Internment Camps

During World War II, 450,000 captured German, Japanese and Italian soldiers were brought back to prisoner of war camps in the United States. Also, more than 100,000 West Coast Japanese-American citizens were forced into internment camps across the United States.

German POW Items

Item	Value
Certificate of Achievement, completing elementary English course	$38-$45
Canteen Coupon, 1 cent, Camp Como, MS	$25-$30
Canteen Coupon, 2 cents, Camp Robinson, AR	$25-$30
Canteen Coupon, 5 cents, Camp Polk, LA	$25-$30
Canteen Coupon, 10 cents, Camp Rucker, AL	$25-$30
Coupon Cover, Barkeley, TX, POW camp canteen	$10-$16
Coupon Cover, Niagara, NY, POW camp canteen	$10-$16
Drawing, charcoal of German officer, prisoner-signed	$80-$100
Field Manual, "U.S. Basic Guard Duty," 1942	$15-$20
Envelope, POW Camp Exchange, Concordia, KS, 1944	$14-$18
Newspaper, *Der Ruf*, POW printed	$65-$75
Newspaper, *The POW WOW*, POW Camp, Brady, TX, 1955	$40-$50
Photo, press release, 8" x 10", German soldiers sewing uniforms at Fort Meade, MD	$7-$10
Photo, press release, 8" x 10", German soldiers working in a field in Kansas	$7-$10
Poster, FBI Wanted Poster, 10" x 16", 2 escaped Germans, Canadian POW camp, November 1942	$120-$150
Shirt, United States Herringbone, twill, marked "P.W."	$65-$80
Oil Painting, landscape from Camp Grant, IL	$125-$160
Photo Album, chaplain from camp, Trinidad, CO	$175-$225
Postcard, change of address for German POW	$28-$35
Underwear, long johns, marked "P.W. Camp," Robinson, AR	$60-$80
Wood Carving, American eagle shield, prisoner-signed	$55-$75
Wood Carving, German U-Boat, made by prisoner	$95-$125
Work pants, dark blue, marked with white "PW"	$60-$75
Work shirt, dark blue, marked with white "PW"	$60-$75

Italian POW Items

Item	Value
Letter, 303rd Italian Quartermaster Battalion, Camp Shanks, NY, 1945	$27-$33
Patches, worn by Italian POWs, large ones for uniform/small for cap	$60-$75
Postcard, Italian prisoner held at Coolidge, AZ, mailed to Italy	$35-$50
Poster, FBI Wanted Poster, 10" x 16", escaped Italian prisoner, Camp Shanks, NY, 1945	$120-$150
Photo, 8" x 10", Italian POWs working at camp in Riverside, CA	$7-$10
Wood Carving, American eagle shield, prisoner-signed	$55-$75

Japanese-American Internment Items

Item	Value
Christmas Card, sent within camp, Topaz, UT	$60-$75
Duffel Bag, Japanese family ID tags attached	$80-$95
Envelope, War Relocation Authority, Washington, DC, 1943	$22-$25
Newspaper, *Granada Pioneer*, Amache, CO, 1943	$65-$80
Newspaper, *Heart Mountain Sentinel*, 1945	$65-$80
Newspaper, *Manazar Free Press*, California, 1944	$80-$100
Photo ID, internee from camp at Rohwe, AR	$180-$200
Photos, Japanese family, Heart Mountain Internment Camp, 1944	$75-$95
Work Permit, pass from camp at Poston, AZ	$60-$80
Wood Carving, American flag	$70-$90

U.S. POW Items

Package, sent to U.S. POW, returned by censor ($25-$35).

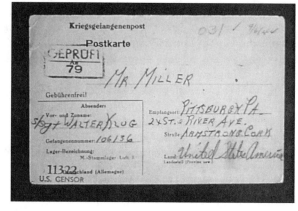

Postcard, sent from German prison camp by U.S. soldier to Pittsburgh ($25-$30).

Top: Coupon Book Cover, Italian POW Camp, Belle Mead, NJ ($12-$18); Bottom: Coupon Cover, Algona, IA, POW camp canteen ($10-$16).

Poster, FBI Wanted Poster, 10" x 16", escaped German, Fort Devens, MA, June 1945 ($130-$160).

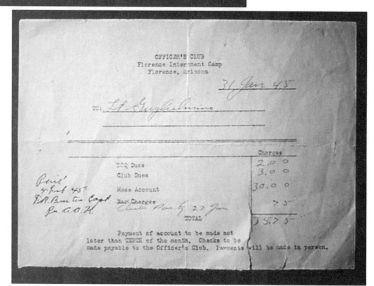

Receipt, officers' club tab, Florence, AZ, internment camp, 1945 ($28-$35).

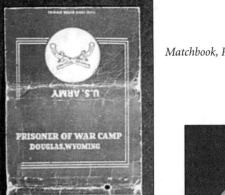

Matchbook, POW Camp, Douglas, WY ($15-$20).

Field Jacket, United States M-1941, second version, marked "P.W." ($80-$100).

Magazine, U.S. News, "POW Camp Report," 1943 ($22-$28).

Poster, 10" x 16", Notice to Aliens of Enemy Nationalities for Western U.S., 1942 ($130-$160).

Poster, 11" x 17", Internment Instructions for Japanese, Sanger, CA, 1942 ($120-$150).

Sheet Music (9" x 12")

Item	Value
10 Great War Songs, Robbins Music Corp., 1944	$10-$15
The Air Corps Song, Capt. Robert Crawford/Carl Fischer, 1939, 1942	$15-$15
Comin' In On a Wing and a Prayer, Harold Adamson/Jimmy McHugh, Robbins Music Corp., 1943	$15-$20
Der Fuehrer's Face from Donald Duck in Nutzi Land, Oliver Wallace, Southern Music Publishing Co., Inc., 1942	$25-$30
I've Been Drafted, Now I'm Drafting You, Lyle Moraine/Chuck Foster, 1941	$10-$15
I Left My Heart at the Stage Door Canteen, from This is the Army, Irving Berlin, 1941	$15-$20
National Defense March, Stanford King, 1942	$5-$10
Praise the Lord and Pass the Ammunition, Frank Loesser, Famous Music Corp., 1942	$20-$25
The Road to Victory, Frank Loesser, Pacific Music Sales, 1943	$10-$15
Song Hits, Song Lyrics Inc., 1942	$5-$10
There's' a Star Spangled Banner Waiving Somewhere, Paul Roberts/Shelby Darnell, Bob Miller, Inc., 1942	$10-$15
They're Either Too Young or Too Old, Warner Bros, 1943	$15-$20
This Is The Army, by Irving Berlin, Army Emergency Relief, 1942	$15-$20
Victory Polka, Samuel Cahn/Jule Styne, Chappell & Co., Inc., 1943	$10-$15
We're Soldiers All, Lee Moller/Emil Goepp, Oahu Publishing Co., 1942	$10-$15
We Must Be Vigilant from When Johnny Comes Marching Home, Edgar Leslie/Joseph Burke, Bregman, Vocco and Conn, Inc., 1942	$10-$15
When the Lights Go On Again (All Over the World), Campbell/Loft, Porgie Pub. N.Y., 1942	$15-$20
The Whiffenpoof Song, from Winged Victory, Moss Hart/Meade Minnigerode/George Pomeroy/Todd Galloway, Miller Music Corp., 1936, 1942	$10-$15
The Yank and a Tank, Everett Bentley/Campbell/Loft, Porgie, Inc. N.Y., 1943	$15-$20

Remember Pearl Harbor, Don Reid/Sammy Kaye, Republic Music Corp., 1941 ($15-$20).

BE A HERO, MY BOY, Mark Minkus/Henry Kane, Patriotic Music Pub. N.Y. ($20-$25).

THEY LIVE FOREVER, Jacques Wolke/Margaret Bristol/G. Schirmer, Inc., N.Y, 1942 ($15-$20).

CHEER UP, UNCLE SAM!, Mark Minkus/Henry Kane, Patriotic Music Pub., N.Y. ($30-$35).

*Wait for Me Mary, Charlie Tobias/Nat Simon/
Henry Tobias, Remick Music Corp., 1942
($15-$20).*

*BE PATIENT, MY LOVE, Mark Minkus/
Henry Kane, Patriotic Music Pub. N.Y.
($15-$20).*

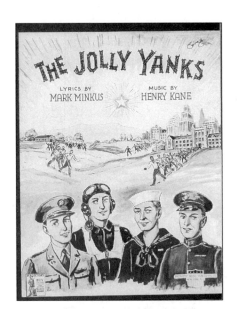

*THE JOLLY YANKS, Mark Minkus/Henry
Kane, Patriotic Music Pub. N.Y. ($15-$20).*

*V for Victory is our Shield, Mark Minkus/
Henry Kane, Patriotic Music Pub. N.Y.
($10-$15).*

*Goodnight Captain Curly-Head, Sam M. Lewis/
Fred E. Ahlert, Ahlert and Lewis, N.Y, 1942
($10-$15).*

*MARCHING AND SINGING, Mark Minkus/
Henry Kane, Patriotic Music Pub. N.Y.
($15-$20).*

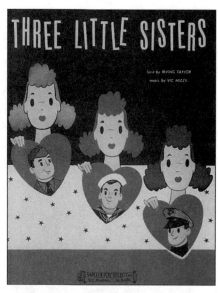

Three Little Sisters, Irving Taylor/Vic Mizzy, Santly-Joy-Select Inc. N.Y, 1942 ($10-$15).

ANY BONDS TODAY?, Irving Berlin/Henry Morgenthau Jr., Secretary of the Treasury, 1941 ($15-$20).

THERE'S A STAR SPANGLED BANNER WAVING SOMEWHERE, Paul Roberts/Shelby Darnell, Bob Miller Inc., 1942 ($10-$15).

HERE COMES THE NAVY, Lt. Com. Oaks, Shapiro/Bernstein Co. N.Y, 1943 ($15-$20).

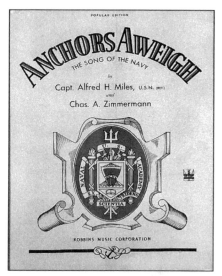

ANCHORS AWEIGH, Capt. Miles/Zimmermann, Robbins Music Corp., 1943 ($15-$20).

BELL BOTTOM TROUSERS, Moe Jaffe, Santly-Joy Inc., 1944 ($15-$20).

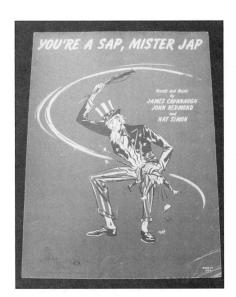

You're A Sap, Mister Jap, Cavanaugh, Mills Music, NY, 1941 ($20-$25).

American Victory Songs, Eckstein, Carl Fisher Inc. NY, 1942 ($10-$15).

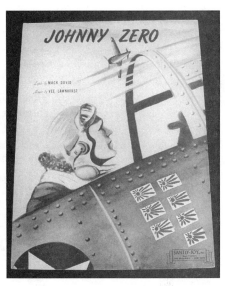

Johnny Zero, Lawnhurst, Santly-Joy, NY, 1943 ($10-$15).

Rosie The Riveter, Evans, Paramount Music, NY, 1942 ($15-$20).

We're Gonna Have to Slap the Dirty Little Jap, Miller Inc., 1941 ($25-$30).

We Did It Before and We Can Do It Again, Cantor, Witmark & Sons, NY, 1941 ($10-$15).

Sports

Item	Value
Banner, Cloth, "Chicago Cubs," 66" x 102", RWB, 16 stars/stripes, "Back the War Effort/Buy Bonds," 1944	$1,000-$1,200
Baseball, signed, "Joe DiMaggio, 7th Army Air Force," Reach American League Ball, 1944	$2,000-$2,500
Book, "How to Play 2nd base," red and blue, large "V," All-Star Services, Gehringer, 1943	$45-$55
Broadside, cardboard, Boxing Exhibition, 16" x 27", green/black, Willie Pep/Sandy Saddler, "Navy War Relief Fund," 1943	$250-$275
Button, celluloid, 3/4" black/red, "Ask Me, Johnny Mize for Democracy," 1942	$75-$100
Button, celluloid, 1-1/4", yellow/black, "Joe DiMaggio Victory Club," Buitoni Macaroni Food Corp.	$75-$100
Comic Book, "True Sport," DiMaggio, Soldier, Sailor, Marine, Vol. #1, 1945	$175-$200
Decal, Advertisement, 10" x 23-1/2", litho, "Sammy Baugh Passing for Uncle Sam," Rawlings, 1943	$125-$150
Guide, Press, baseball, 4" x 8", brown, St. Louis Browns, American League, planes/ships/artillery, 1944	$150-$175
Jacket, Yankee Stadium Ushers, blue wool, size 44, "Stars/Stripes" patch on left sleeve, McGregor, 1945	$500-$650
Jersey, San Francisco Seals with "V" Patch, 1943	$2,000-$2,500
Photo, signed, "Ted Williams," black/white, 8" x 10", U.S. Marines uniform/J.H. Williams Certificate	$375-$400
Pomade, Hair Dressing, "Joe Louis," 5-1/2" x 1-1/4", round yellow with orange/black, "Minuteman—Buy Savings Bonds," sticker, Joe Louis Products, 1942	$175-$200
Postcard, 3-1/2" x 5", sepia tone, "Sgt. Joe Louis"	$50-$75
Poster, Coca-Cola, 20" x 27", "Relax…Take It Easy," two baseball players/serviceman, Coke, 1942	$400-$500
Press Pass, 4" x 6-1/4", yellow/black, Soldier Field, MacArthur Image, Chicago, 1945	$75-$100
Program, "Ice Follies," RWB, Sonia Henie Skating Through USA Flag, Shipstad/Johnson, 1944	$125-$150
Program, Football, Championship Playoff, Rams vs. Redskins, Uncle Sam running with football, 1945	$150-$175
Program, World Series, 9" x 12", Yankees vs. Cardinals, 1943	$125-$150
Razor, Gillette, 2-1/4" x 3-3/4" x 1-1/8", "World Series Special Tech Razor," red Rolfe/Uncle Sam, 1942	$175-$200
Scorecard, baseball, Athletics, black/red, Uncle Sam shaking hands with Connie Mack, 1943	$65-$75
Scorecard, baseball, Oakland Oaks, Pacific Coast League, RWB, "On to Victory," planes/artillery/stars and stripes, 1944	$45-$55
Ticket, "Hollywood Park Race Track," 2-1/4" x 6", gray, "V"	$50-$75
Ticket, baseball, "All-Star Game," sponsor Armed Forces Equipment Fund, 1944	$250-$275
Wrapper, baseball, 8" x 8-1/4", RWB, American League baseball, "Wrapped to Conserve," Reach Corp., 1942	$250-$275

Scorebooks, from left: 1943 San Francisco Seals ($75-$100); 1943 Phillies ($60-$75); 1943 Oakland ($60-$75).

Scorecard, "OFFICIAL," Comiskey Park, 6" x 9", "It's a Family Affair," "Drink Coca-Cola," 1942 ($35-$45).

Scorecard, "Boost the Rebels," 7" x 11-1/4", Montgomery baseball club, Uncle Sam batting the Axis, Montgomery AL, 1942 ($50-$65).

Program, "Princeton vs. Columbia," pilot's face above football players ($45-$55).

Scorebook, "VICTORY BOUND!", Paratroopers, Battleship, baseball Player, San Francisco Seals, 1945 ($60-$75).

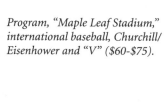

Program, "Gilmore Field," MacArthur, RWB, 1945 ($75-$85).

Program, "College of the Pacific vs. U.S. Pre-Flight School St. Mary's College," 1944 ($60-$75).

Program, "Maple Leaf Stadium," international baseball, Churchill/ Eisenhower and "V" ($60-$75).

Transit Ride Pass/Patches, pass shows football player kicking in front of "V," 1942 ($10-$15 each).

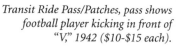

Stamps, Stickers, Decals & Labels

These patriotic symbols were styled after postage stamps and came in a multitude of sizes and shapes. They were usually lithographed on adhesive paper or made into decals and then stuck to envelopes, stationary, book covers, postcards or any smooth surface to show support for the war effort and rally our troops abroad. Colorful art images with captions such as "Buy Bonds," "Plant a Victory Garden," and "Save Food and Gas" were among the thousands that were produced. Like many homefront collectibles, these stamps and stickers are bargain-priced and provide collectors a wonderful insight into wartime America.

Item	Value

Stamp Album, "Famous War Posters," 2" x 3", multi colors, 50 reproductions of the most famous WWII Posters produced by the Office of War Information. Stamps and album holder distributed by Associated Dealers. This set is considered by collectors as the most desired Cinderella stamp set of the period, 1944, each..$7-$10

1. LET'S HIT 'EM, DON'T WAIT—CHOOSE THE NAVY
2. KEEP 'EM FLYING
3. WANT ACTION? JOIN THE MARINE CORPS
4. BUILD AND FIGHT IN THE NAVY SEABEES
5. YOU BET I'M GOING BACK TO SEA!
6. MERCHANT SEAMEN DELIVER
7. JOIN THE WACS NOW
8. ENLIST IN THE WAVES
9. BE A MARINE…FREE A MARINE TO FIGHT
10. ENLIST IN THE COAST GUARD SPARS NOW
11. BECOME A NURSE, YOUR COUNTRY NEEDS YOU
12. FIGHTING MEN NEED NURSES
13. VOLUNTEER RED CROSS NURSE'S AIDE
14. TAKE A RED CROSS NURSING COURSE
15. WORK ON A FARM, JOIN THE U.S. CROP CORPS
16. ENROLL NOW WITH AWVS
17. DO HIS JOB HE LEFT BEHIND
18. JOIN WOMEN'S LAND ARMY
19. I'M COUNTING ON YOU
20. A CARELESS WORD…A NEEDLESS LOSS
21. A CARELESS WORD…ANOTHER CROSS
22. A CARELESS WORD…A NEEDLESS SINKING
23. OURS…TO FIGHT FOR, FREEDOM FROM WANT
24. OURS…TO FIGHT FOR, FREEDOM FROM FEAR
25. SAVE FREEDOM OF WORSHIP, BUY WAR BONDS
26. SAVE FREEDOM OF SPEECH WANT
27. SALVAGE VICTORY, THROW YOUR SCRAP INTO THE FIGHT
28. SAVE YOUR CANS, HELP PASS AMMUNITION
29. YOUR METAL IS ON THE ATTACK, KEEP IT COMING
30. YOUR METAL FIGHTS THE JAPS, KEEP IT COMING
31. SAVE WASTES FATS AND EXPLOSIVES
32. SAVE RUBBER, CHECK YOUR TIRES NOW
33. GROW YOUR OWN, CAN YOUR OWN
34. DO WITH LESS, SO THEY'LL HAVE ENOUGH
35. AMERICANS FISHING FLEET AND MEN—ASSETS TO VICTORY
36. PLANT A VICTORY GARDEN
37. THE FREEDOM OF THE SEAS IS IN YOUR HANDS

38. A GOOD SOLDIER STICKS TO HIS POST
39. BUY WAR BONDS
40. BUY WAR BONDS—3rd WAR LOAN
41. DOING ALL YOU CAN BROTHER? BUY WAR BONDS
42. BACK THE ATTACK, BUY WAR BONDS
43. SULLIVAN BROTHERS, THEY DID THEIR PART
44. GIVE ONE A YEAR, WAR CHEST
45. YOUR BLOOD CAN SAVE HIM
46. HELP SOMEONE YOU KNOW WHEN YOU GIVE TO THE USO
47. UNITED NATIONS FIGHT FOR FREEDOM
48. FIRST TO FIGHT—UNITED CHINA RELIEF
49. AMERICAN JUNIOR RED CROSS
50. AMERICANS ALL-LET'S FIGHT FOR VICTORY

Item	Value
Decal, "Defense Victory Ride," 4" round, orange/blue, 1941	$15-$20
Decal, "Don't Discuss Troop Movements," 3-1/2" x 7", RWB	$20-$25
Decal, "I Bought Defense Bonds, Did You?", 3-1/2" x 4-3/4", RWB	$15-$20
Decal "Inevitable Triumph, So Help Us God," 3-1/2" x 4-1/2", multicolor	$20-$25
Decal, "Keep 'Em Flying," 4-3/4" x 5-1/8", multi colors, Poster Stamp Press	$25-$35
Decal, "My Son Serving," 3" x 4", Statue of Liberty, red and blue	$15-$20
Decal, "On to Victory," 4-3/4" x 5", red and blue, MacArthur, 1942	$20-$25
Decal, "Rush for Victory," 2-1/2" x 3-1/2", RWB, Tompkins	$7-$10
Decal, "U-Before V," 3" x 3-1/2", RWB, Atlanta	$10-$15
Decal, "V for Victory," 3" x 5-1/4", red and blue/silver foil, die-cut	$15-$20
Decal, "V-Morse Code," 4" x 4", RWB, HiBrand	$10-$15
Decal, "Victory, Thumbs Up," 3-1/2" x 3-1/2", RWB	$15-$20
Decal, "We Will Win," 4-1/2" round, RWB, Roosevelt, V	$25-$35
Decal, "War Worker," 3-1/2" x 5", RWB, Logging & Lumber	$15-$20
Label, "V-Bread," 1-3/4" x 3", RWB, U.S. Govt. Standards	$7-$10
Label, "Victory—Morse Code," 3" x 4", red and blue, Ever Ready, 1942	$15-$20
Stamp, "Cotton Week," 2" x 2-1/2", RWB	$5-$7
Stamp, "Flowers for Morale," 1-1/2" x 2", RWB	$5-$7
Stamp, "Free Speech Doesn't Mean Careless Talk," Seagram	$5-$7
Stamp, "Loose Lips Might Sink Ships," 1-1/2" x 2", Seagram	$5-$7
Stamp, "Make Saps Out of the Japs," 1-1/2" x 1-3/4", RWB	$7-$10

Stamps, block of 10, miniature posters, "Keep 'em Rolling," "Full Speed Ahead," "Back Him Up," etc., for block ($25-$35).

Item	**Value**
Stamp, "National Feed Week," 2" x 2-1/2", RWB, 1941	$5-$7
Stamp, "No Room For Rumors," 1-1/2" x 2", Seagram	$5-$7
Stamp, "Pearl Harbor Bond," 2-1/2" x 3-1/4", red and blue	$5-$7
Stamp, "Plant Seeds For Victory," 1-1/2" x 2", black/green	$5-$7
Stamp, "Put Muscle in His Arms," 1-1/2" x 2", RWB	$5-$7
Stamp, "Remember You're American," 2" x 3", RWB	$7-$10
Stamp, "Save, Serve, Conserve," 1-3/4" x 2-1/8", RWB, Andrews	$5-$7
Stamp, "Smash the Japs," 1-1/2" x 1-3/4", RWB	$5-$7
Stamp, "Speed War Production," 1-1/2" x 2", RWB, Elliott-Lewis	$5-$7
Stamp, "Stop Rumors," 1-1/2" x 2", Seagram	$5-$7
Stamp, "Tools and Weapons," 2-1/8" x 3", black/white	$5-$7
Stamp, "V For Victory," 1-3/4" x 2-1/8", RPH, Manhattan Life Insurance	$5-$7
Stamp, "V Paper Is Essential," 1-1/2" x 2", red and blue/silver foil	$5-$7
Stamp, "Value-One Cent," 1" x 1", blue/white, Idaho, 1943	$3-$5

Stickers, Patriotic (5), flags, marines and soldiers, each ($5-$10).

Photo Stamps, block of 12, "Hurry up! This is for a Soldier," RWB, 1-1/2" x 2-1/2", for block ($20-$25).

Stationery

Open Stationery Kit, "Thinking of You," triple foldout, beautiful blonde on her side ($45-$55).

(Front cover of above) Stationery Kit, "Thinking of You," soldier sitting on foot locker ($45-$55).

Stationery, cartoon types, "V" theme ($20-$35 each).

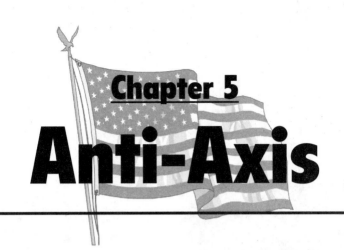

Anti-Axis propaganda was used to not only instill fear and hatred, but also to portray the enemy as silly fools, powerless cartoons that are to be laughed at and mocked. Some of the most sought after WWII home-front collectibles are the comical portrayals of Hitler, Tojo and Mussolini. These Anti-Axis items came in the form of postcards, box games, sheet music, matchbooks, posters, envelopes, stickers and letterhead as well as toys, banks, dolls, figures, mechanical arcade attractions, ash trays, toothpick holders and pin cushions.

Arcade Games: There were several categories of penny-arcade games. First, there were games that insulted the enemy, "Bomb Hitler," "Smack the Jap" or "Poison the Rats." There were shooting galleries and penny drops that used Hitler's, Mussolini's or Tojo's faces for targets. Another category were games that sank enemy battleships, and shot down enemy planes by releasing gum balls as bombs or firing simulated machine guns. A third category were machines decorated with patriotic slogans and homefront motifs that proclaimed the proceeds from playing the games were going to be donated to support the war effort. The "V" symbol, "Buy Savings Bonds" and "Uncle Sam," were frequently used to decorate these marvelous arcade games.

Dish, comic, "Careless Talk Costs Lives," sailor in bathtub with woman, "and this is how a torpedo works, Miss Fothergill," Hitler listening from toilet ($75-$95).

Item	Value
Ashtray, "Caught in the Allies Web…Drop Your Ashes On Old Nasty," 5" dia., Hitler's face in web with spider approaching, Crown Devon, England	$125-$150
Bookmark, "Careless Matches Aid the Axis!", 2-1/2" x 7", orange/black, "Prevent Forest Fires," Japanese soldier with lit match	$25-$35
Comic Book, "All Winners," The Human Torch, Captain America, The Sub Mariner, Axis powers being stomped on by the heroes	$300-$400
Display, two paper mache musicians with violin and drum, pulling a sting to makes them move, 23" x 15" x 25", "Buy Bonds, Beat the Axis"	$950-$1,100
Display Board, "Nuts," 22-1/4" x 22-1/4", black/tan, Hitler/Mussolini/Stalin, Oliver V. Chadwick, 1940	$175-$225
Envelope, "All Together Work or Fight for Victory," Axis in nutcracker, large "V," 1944	$10-$15
Envelope, "Clear the Tracks," train after Axis gang, Minkus, 1942	$15-$20
Envelope, "The Eagle Will Get the Rattlesnake," eagle with two-headed Axis snake, 1942	$15-$20
Envelope, "The Enemy is Listening," with Hitler Ear, Warner Pursell, 1945	$15-$20
Envelope, "First Dictator to Fall Benito Mussolini," with Mussolini and Goat, 1944	$10-$15
Envelope, "Greetings from the US Coast Guard," Crush Japanese Menace, Destroy Nazism, Crosby, 1944	$15-$20
Envelope, "Help Fill This Reserved Space/Buy More War Bonds," Mussolini grave with space for Hitler, G.D.W, 1944	$10-$15

Item	**Value**
Envelope, "Let's Go USA," Hawaii back stabbed by Japanese flag, Artcraft, 1943	$10-$15
Envelope, "Let's Go USA," RWB, Axis as flies, Statue of Liberty, Artcraft, 1943	$10-$15
Envelope, "Let's Go USA," Uncle Sam's boot on Axis snakes, Artcraft, 1943	$10-$15
Envelope, "Not So Fast Adolf," eagle with Hitler in claws, Minkus 1942	$15-$20
Envelope, "Not to Tokyo: The Story of the B's," with bee hive & B-24s, 1944	$15-$20
Envelope, "Stamp 'em Out," Uncle Sam's boot on heads of Axis, Minkus, 1943	$15-$20
Envelope, "Three of a Kind from Rome-Berlin-Tokyo," Axis leaders as animals, Crosby, 1943	$15-$20
Envelope, "Two Bad Eggs Help Smash 'em, Buy Warm Bonds," Tojo/Adolph, 1944	$15-$20
Envelope, "What Hitler Prays for!", multi war messages homefront and Hitler, Boone, 1944	$15-$20
Envelope, "Yaaa Who Voodt Belief It," Hitler as donkey, 1943	$15-$20
Envelope, "Yes Adolph, We're Coming!", RWB, soldier chasing Hitler into the Alps, 1944	$15-$20
Envelope, "Your Empty Tubes Will Furnish Tin to Can the Axis," Axis gang running, 1943	$15-$20
Figures, chalkware, Axis set, Hitler—13", Tojo—11", Mussolini—12", standing with necks bent as if hanged	$750-$1,000
Game, "Put Hitler in the Dog House," 3-1/2" x 4-1/2", red/black/white, Zen, 1942	$75-$95
Jap Hunting License, "Good for the Open Season on Yellow Belly Japs," 3-1/4" x 2-1/2", black/blue	$30-$35
Lunch Bag, paper, 6-1/2" x 13-1/2", Axis powers cooked in a kettle, "Save on House Heat and Help Make Things Hotter for Hitler," "Fuel is Needed to Build Weapons"	$35-$45
Magazine, *Colliers*, July 25, 1942, monkey as Japanese pulling rickshaw carrying Hitler as monkey	$45-$55
Magazine, *Divide and Conquer*, U.S. Govt., 1942	$20-$25
Matchbook, "Smash the Axis," American Match Co.	$15-$20
Matchbook, "Step on It, Work to Crush the Axis," Inta-State Press	$15-$20
Matchbook, "Swat the Axis, Save Waste Paper," Armory Match	$10-$15
Matchbook, "There's a Happy Jap for Every Gap on the Production Line," Universal Match	$15-$20
Matchbook, "Total Eclipse: Buy More Bonds," Inta-State Press	$15-$20
Novelty, envelope and insert, 3-1/2" x 5-1/2", "Heel Hitler," lift the toilet seat cover and you dunk Hitler into the bowl, DR and Co., 1942	$35-$45
Panties, "Shoot the Pants Off the Japs," 3-1/2" x 2-1/2", paper, pink/black	$25-$35
Pin/Booklet, "Eat to Beat the Devil," Hitler with horns being punched, pin is cello 1-1/2", for set	$30-$45
Pin, cello, button, "Amelican Yes!…No Japanese!", 1-1/4", RWB	$35-$50
Pin, cello, button, "Be Calm, Be Alert, You Won't Get Hurt," blue/white	$25-$35
Pin, cello, button, "Exterminate These 3 Rats," 1-1/4", B/W, Mussolini/Hitler/Tojo	$25-$35
Pin, cello, button, "Halt Hitler," 5/8", blue/white, Star of David (Jewish star)	$35-$50
Pin, cello, button, "Italy, Germany, and Japan, Can We Lick Them All? You Bet We Can!", 1-1/4", RWB	$25-$35
Pin, cello, button, "Japan Wanted for Murder," 1-1/4", R/W	$25-$35
Pin, cello, button, "Jap Hunting License: Open Season No Limit," 1-1/4", blue/rimmed in white	$50-$65
Pin, cello, button, "Keep Em Flying, Keep Em Sailing, Keep Democracy From Failing," 1-1/4", blue/white	$25-$35
Pin, cello, button, "Kick 'em in the Axis," 1-1/4", RWB	$25-$35
Pin, cello, button, "Let's Blast the Japs Off the Map," 1-1/4", yellow with black	$35-$45
Pin, cello, button, "Let's Pull Together," 1-1/2", multicolor, anti-Hitler mechanical with lever that raises and lowers slotted Hitler image over trailing Uncle Sam's hanging rope	$75-$100
Pin, cello, button, "Let's Set the Rising Sun," 1-1/4", RWB	$35-$45
Pin, cello, button, "Moider Dem Japs," 1-1/4", blue/white	$35-$45
Pin, cello, button, "Pack Up Japan the Yanks are Coming," 1-1/4", blue/white	$35-$45
Pin, cello, button, "Slap the Jap," tin tab, white rimmed in red	$35-$45
Pin, cello, button, "To Hell with Hirohito," 1-1/4", blue/white	$35-$45
Pin, cello, button, "To Hell with Hitler," 1-1/4", B/W	$35-$45
Pin, cello, button, "To Hell with Hitler," goldtone frame, red/white/gold	$50-$65
Pin, cello, button, "To Hell with Mussie," 1-1/4", blue/white	$35-$45
Pin, cello, button, "U.S. has the Axis on the Run," 1-1/4", RWB	$25-$35
Pin, cello, button, "We'll Bomb Each Jap Right Off the Map," RWB	$35-$50
Pin, cello, button, "We'll Pay Them Back for Their Sneak Attack!", 1-1/4", RWB	$35-$50
Pin, cello, button, "We're in It and We'll Win It," 1-1/4", blue/white	$15-$20
Pin, cello, button, "Where is Mussolini?", RWB	$25-$35

Item	**Value**
Pin, cello, button, "You Asked for It Japan," 1-1/4", RWB	$20-$30
Postcard, "Blackout of the Rising Sun," litho, Aviation Comic Series	$5-$10
Postcard, "Bundles for Hitler, Mussolini, Tojo," Beals	$5-$10
Postcard, "DER PHEWRER," b/w photo Hitler in toilet yelling for Benito	$10-$15
Postcard, "Heil Hitler," b/w photo, dog urinating on Hitler photo	$15-$20
Postcard, "Hitler War Fund," b/w photo, Zipper Novelty & Joke Shop, 1942,	$10-$15
Postcard, "I'm Bringing Home the Bacon," linen, Beals,	$5-$10
Postcard, "It's too quiet for him around here, so he's trying to stir up action," Private Berger Series, Graycraft	$5-$10
Postcard, "Just a Little Something to Remember Pearl Harbor," linen, Tichnor Bros., 1942	$5-$10
Postcard, "Like a Rat in His Trap," b/w photo, Hitler in jail	$10-$15
Postcard, "No Pork Until These Pigs are Killed," black/white, Hitler/Tojo/Mussolini	$5-$10
Postcard, "Puzzle: Which is the Skunk?", linen, Beals,	$10-15
Postcard, "The Boys Enjoy Playing that Game More Now," linen, Series T Army, Colourpicture Publication	$10-15
Postcard, "Those Japs Will Soon Be Slap Happy," linen, Tichnor Bros, 1942	$10-$15
Postcard, "Three of a Kind," b/w photo, Hilborn Novelty, 1942	$10-$15
Postcard, "To My Brave Soldier Boy," linen, Colourpicture Publication	$10-$15
Postcard, "We're Giving 'em a Big WAC," linen, Beals,	$5-$10
Postcard, "We're Letting Him Have It Right Square in the Butt," Beals,	$5-$10
Postcard, "We are Giving These Yellow-Bellied Japs What's Comin to Them and How," linen, Tichnor Bros, 1942,	$10-$15
Postcard, "You Tellum Soldier Boy," Morale Booster Series A, Colourpicture Publication, 1942	$10-$15
Poster, "Prevent Sabotage," 16" x 20", red/black/yellow, Consolidated Edison Co., 1942	$75-$85
Poster, "Uncle Sam, War on Waste," 26" x 32", RWB, Scott Washroom Advisory Service, #1173	$100-$125
Poster, "V Mail is Speed Mail," RWB, U.S. Govt., 11" x 30"	$85-$95
Poster, "You've Done Your Bit/Now Do Your Best," "Buy War Bonds," RWB, 10" x 52"	$75-$100
Table Cloth, 45" x 50", cotton, various anti-Axis comic themes including Rommel being pushed into the sea	$125-$150

Pincushion, reversible from Hitler to Tojo and Togo to Hitler, 5" high, cushion at side ($225-$250).

Pins, cello buttons ($25-$35 each).

Heels, shoe replacements, "O'Sullivan's Safety Cushion," 4-1/2" x 3", box, Japanese soldier with green face running ($40-$50).

Poster, "You Help the Enemy if You Buy Black Market Gas," 8-1/2" x 11", buck-tooth Japanese soldier ($30-$40).

Matchbook, "Step on it!", Uncle Sam stepping on Mussolini, Tojo, Hitler, "Work to Crush the Axis ($5-$8).

Toilet Seat Cover, 3-1/2" x 5-1/2", "See What Happens to Adolf!", "Heel Hitler," D.R. and Co., 1942 ($35-$45).

Matchbook, "Total Eclipse!", face of Japanese soldier, "Buy More Bonds" ($5-$8).

Pin, cello button, "Jap Hunting License," "Open Season—No Limit," red/white ($35-$45).

Figure, Hitler as Skunk, 3-1/2" x 2-1/2", carved wood with swastika on chest ($150-$200).

Figure, Hitler as Skunk, 3-1/2" x 2-1/2", plaster with swastika on chest ($150-$175).

Punch Board, "Take a Punch," 7-3/4" x 9-1/4", Hitler face in left corner, red/white/black Hamilton Mfg., MN ($35-$45).

Ashtrays: "Jam Your Cigarette Butts On This" Skunk [Hitler], Vulture [Mussolini], Rat [Tojo], glass ($195-$225 for set).

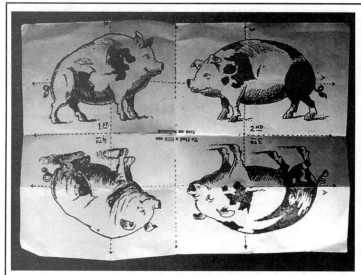

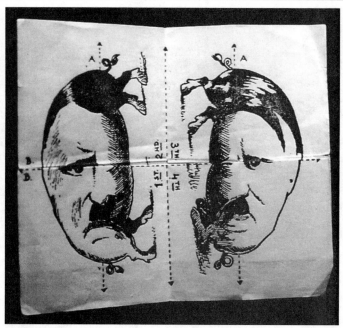

Game, "Find the Pig," fold the paper game, 8-1/2" x 11" ($5-$10).

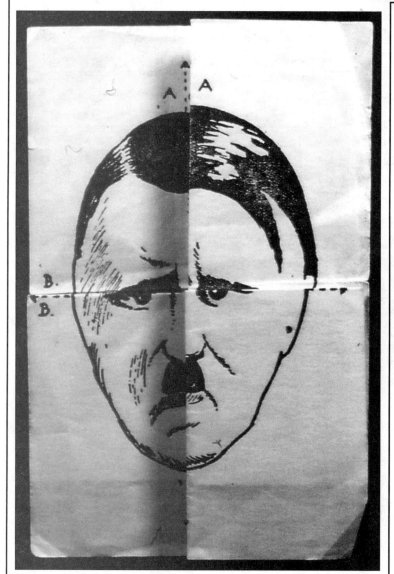

License, "License to Hunt Japanese," 7" x 9", tan/gray/white, "Open Season, No Limit" ($85-$100).

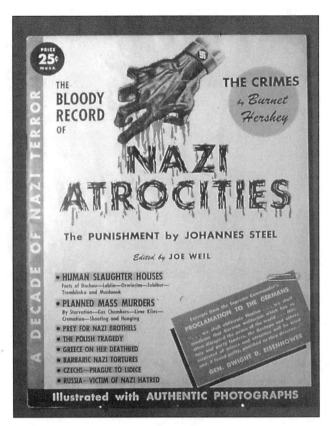

Ashtray, chamberpot, ceramic Hitler face at bottom, 1-1/2" x 2", "Hitler in Poland" ($75-$95).

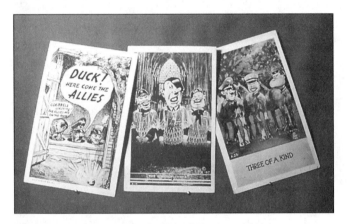

Postcards, black/white, 3-1/2" x 5-1/2" ($5-$10 each).

Booklet, "Nazi Atrocities," 8-1/2" x 11", bloody hand, Joe Weil ($20-$30).

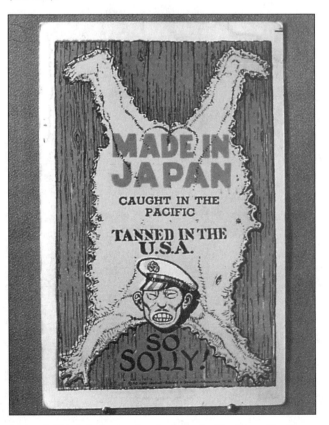

Pin Cushion, chalkware, Hitler bending over, 6-1/4" high, "Stick a Pin in the Axis" ($200-$250).

Postcard, "Made in Japan, Caught in the Pacific, Tanned in the U.S.A, So Solly!", Japanese sailor as rug ($5-$10).

Coffee Cup, half-cup, ceramic, 2-1/2" x 1-1/2", Stalin with pipe "An Oddity: Two faced Half-Assed," "To My Half Ass Friend" ($75-$85).

Napkin, paper, 4" x 4", RWB, Uncle Sam spanking Tojo ($15-$20).

Blotters: ($5-$10 each).

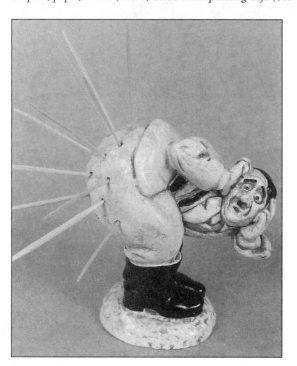 

Toothpick Holder, comic Hitler bending over, plaster, 4-1/2" x 2-1/2" ($275-$350).

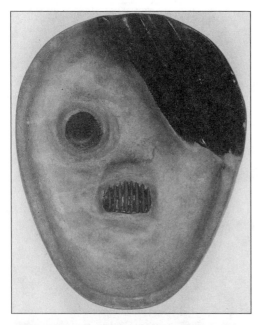

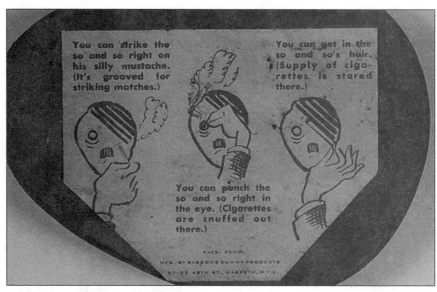

Left and above: Ashtray, comic Hitler face, 5" x 6", fleshtone, designed to light matches on mustache, Bassons Dummy Products, NY, 1942 ($225-$250).

Ashtray, comic Mussolini face, 5" x 2", fleshtone, Bassons Dummy Products, NY ($200-$225).

Figure, Hitler's head in form of walnut, 2" high, "Crack This Nut," plaster shirt and stand ($225-$250).

Figure, Hitler in form of monkey, 4" high, composition, swastika on arm ($200-$225).

Pin Cushion, comic Hitler bending over, 4-3/4" high, "Hotzi Notzi" tag attached, Bassons Dummy Products, NY, 1941 ($200-$225).

Figure, Hitler as skunk, 2-1/2" x 5", plaster ($185-$225).

Postcard, "Jap War Lords," 3-1/2" x 5-1/2", "Donations for Japs," dog using chamber pot, H. Wachtman, 1942 ($20-$30).

Display Card, "Let's Pull Together/ Hang Hitler," 11" x 13-1/2", cello buttons (no buttons) ($100-$125).

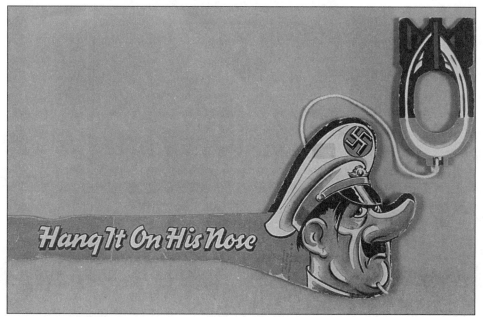

Game, ring toss, cardboard in the shape of Hitler's face, "Hang it on His Nose" 6" x 14", Modern Novelties Inc., OH ($85-$100).

Greeting Cards, cartoons ($15-$20 each).

Postcards, (8) linen, Anti-Axis, cartoons ($10-$15 each).

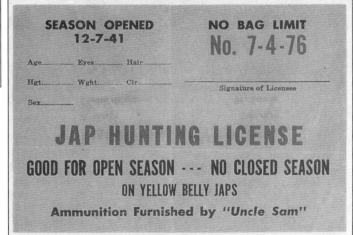

Jap Hunting License ($35-$50).

Envelope, "Wanted for Murder," Axis powers ($10-$15).

Ashtray, "Going, Going, Gone," 5-1/2" x 5", chalkware busts of Tojo, Hitler, Mussolini, C De Spelty Co ($275-$350).

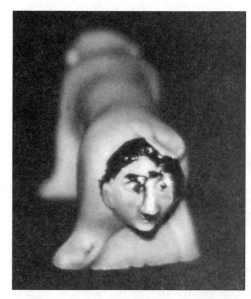

Dog, ceramic, 6" long, Hitler's face on butt ($125-$150).

Figure, composition, Hitler with right arm raised, 2-1/2" x 2-1/2", Carga, 1941 ($150-$200).

Ashtray, Hitler with open mouth, 4" x 7", metal, Basson ($125-$150).

Ashtrays, plaster, Tojo, Mussolini, Hitler labels on bases and poem on back ($550-$700 for set).

Poster, "Get in the Scrap," 33" x 60", kids throwing a pot at Japanese soldier, "Give Your Old Metal and Rubber Now!" ($200-$250).

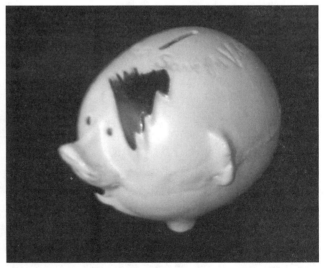

Bank, piggy Hitler's face, pressed wood, yellow, "Make Him Squeal, Save for Victory" around coin slot ($200-$225).

Matchbooks, anti-Axis themes ($5-$15 each).

Arcade Game, penny drop, 10-1/2" x 12-1/2" x 21", "Smash a Jap," "Keep 'em Bombing," can drop 25 pennies in 5 slots at once ($1,800-$2,500).

Arcade Game, ball drops into Hitler's mouth, 10-1/4" x 15-1/2" x 23-1/2", "Poison This Rat," dot designed, Groetelton Tool Co ($3,500-$5,000).

Figure, Hitler skunk, chalkware, anti-Japanese rear end, 5" x 5", "Japan's Rising Sun" on rear ($175-$250).

Arcade Game, penny drop, 6" x 12" x 14", "Bomb Hitler," Coin Machine Co. of America, Indiana ($1,200-$2,000).

Souvenir Program, Sugar Bowl, 8-1/4" x 10-3/4", Alabama vs. Duke, Uncle Sam kicking Tojo seated on Hitler, Jan 1, 1945 ($65-$85).

Poster, "Our Carelessness: Their Secret Weapon," Hitler/Tojo faces above forest fire, 22" x 28", State Forest Service ($225-$275).

Greeting Cards, cartoons, Tojo and Hitler ($25-$30 each).

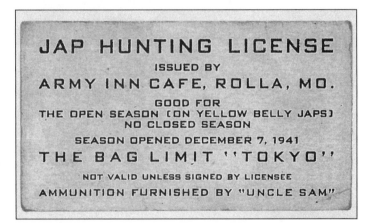

Jap Hunting License ($35-$50).

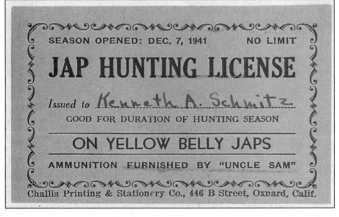

Jap Hunting License ($35-$50).

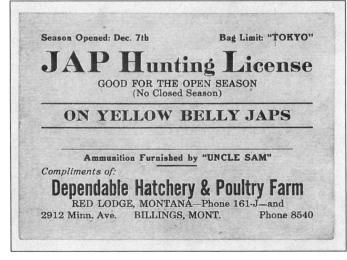

Jap Hunting License ($35-$50).

Jap Hunting License ($35-$50).

Chapter 6
Civilian Defense

Civilian Defense gave this country's civilian population a sense of real pride and purpose knowing that every man, woman and child could do his or her part for the war effort. The threat of an enemy invasion impacted everyone's life from coast-to-coast. From learning to fight fires and give first aid, spotting aircraft, delivering messages, and preparing emergency food and housing, more than 10 million volunteers took an active part.

The Office of Civilian Defense (OCD) produced a multitude of items for its volunteers and the general public, such as uniforms, helmets, guidebooks and pamphlets, gas masks and emergency medical supplies, posters and stickers, all of which are very collectible today.

Light Bulbs, blackout type, from left: Washbase standard; Washbase lamp; and Westinghouse indoor, War Department Standard ($35-$45 each).

Booklet, "800 Ways to Save and Serve," 9" x 6", Manchester Federal, 1943 ($15-$20).

Booklet, "Home Defense Health Course," 7" x 5", Makers of Lysol, 1941 ($10-$15).

Item	**Value**
Badge, Defense Plant Safety Committee Aid, 1-1/2" x 2", metal frame, insert to put photo ID	$25-$35
Banner, window, "War Worker," 8" x 11", RWB	$35-$45
Book Holder, "Vinyl Ration Book Holder," plastic, 6-1/2" x 4-3/4"	$15-$20
Booklet, "69 Ration Recipes for Meat," Armour Co, 1942	$10-$15
Booklet, "AMERICA 1st ADDRESS BOOK," Charles Lindbergh, 6-3/4" x 4", 1941	$10-$15
Booklet, "America on Guard," 6-3/4" x 5-1/2", Uniforms and Insignia, Rand McNally, 1941	$10-$15
Booklet, "BARNUM'S GUIDE TO CIVILIAN DEFENSE," stickers, 10-1/4" x 9-1/4", Barnum's	$5-$8
Booklet, "Betty Crocker Menu & Shopping Guide," General Mills, 1943	$10-$15
Booklet, "DIVISIONAL INSIGNIA," 4-1/8" x 2-1/2", sleeve and shoulder patches of the Army and Marines, Rope Co., 1945	$5-$10
Booklet, "FUEL-GAS EMERGENCY," Southern California Gas Company, 6" x 3-1/2"	$5-$7
Booklet, Guide To U.S. Warships, "Baur's Aunt Hannah's Bread," 1943	$10-$15
Booklet, "Halt," 7-1/2" x 5-1/2", Crestwood Publishing Co, 1943	$10-$15
Booklet, "How to Make a Victory Garden," Akron Fork & Hoe Co., 1943	$10-$15
Booklet, "How to Preserve Victory Garden Vegetables," Standard Oil	$10-$15
Booklet, "The Home Volunteer's Defense Manual," 1942	$15-$20
Booklet, "IDENTIFICATION BOOKLET," 4" x 2-1/2", soldier/sailor/WAC, Borden's Farm Products	$5-$10
Booklet, "Practical Home Nursing" 9" x 5-3/4", William I. Fishbein.	$10-$15
Booklet, "Shoulder Patches," 10-1/2" x 8-1/2", Wolf Appleton	$20-$25
Booklet, "VICTORY GARDENS, How-When-What to Plant," RWB, Board of Education, New Haven	$10-$15
Booklet, "War Birds of the U.S.A.", 7-1/4" x 7-1/8", plane identification, shows eagle flying with U.S. planes, RWB, Filen's Men's Clothing Store	$10-$15
Booklet, "War Work," 8-1/2" x 5-1/2", General Mills, 1943	$15-$20
Booklet, "Wartime Cookbook," by Bradley, World Publishing, 1943	$10-$15
Booklet, "WARTIME Fuel Gas EMERGENCY" 6" x 3-1/2", Southern California Gas Co.	$5-$10
Booklet, "Wartime Guide Book for the Home," Popular Science, 1942	$10-$15
Booklet, "What Can I Do?", 7-3/4" x 5-1/2", Civil Defense Publication	$15-$20
Booklet, "You Can Defend America," 9" x 6", Judd & Detweiler, Inc., 1942	$15-$20
Booklet, "Your Army," 9" x 6", Selective Service, 1942	$10-$15
Cigarette Lighter, 2" x 4", orange/blue box, Foxhole "Blackout," Inco Co	$45-$55
Helmet, Air Raid Warden, 1944 version with large head area, air raid insignia on front, white	$40-$50
First Aid Pouch, 5", drawstring, khaki canvas, 1942	$20-$30
Folder, "7th War Loan," 7-1/2" x 3-1/8", RWB, War Finance Division, 1944	$10-$15
Magazine, *You and the War*, Magazine Publishers of America, 1942	$10-$15
Mailing Box, "Buy More War Bonds," 5" x 6", Beckhard Line Co	$15-$20
Manual, "The AIR RAID SAFETY MANUAL," RWB, by Capt. Burr Leyson, 1943	$10-$15
Pin, celluloid button, "AIR RAID WARDEN," 2-1/4", with serial No., R/W	$25-$35
Pin, celluloid button, "AUXILIARY DEFENSE CORPS," 1-1/4", b&w, "United Aircraft/Messenger" in red	$25-$35
Pin, celluloid button, "AWS VOLUNTEER OBSERVER," 1", "Aircraft Warning Service," with black and orange	$30-$45
Pin, celluloid button, "C.C.N.Y. FOR CIVILIAN DEFENSE," 3/4", "City College of New York," RWB	$25-$35
Pin, celluloid button, "CARPENTER, ESSENTIAL SERVICE," 2-1/4", RWB, "War Production 1943"	$50-$65
Pin, celluloid button, "DEFEND U.S./ALL GUARD," 1-1/4", "U.S. Shield," RWB, with yellow wings	$15-$25
Pin, celluloid button, "FIRST-AID SQUAD," 1", Montgomery, Ala., R/W	$10-$15
Pin, celluloid button, "FOR DEFENSE/PLEASE CARRY SMALL PACKAGES," 1-1/8", RWB	$20-$35
Pin, celluloid button, "NATIONAL DEFENSE DEPENDS ON PERSONAL DEFENSE PRODUCTION," 1", RWB, Shield, "I Wear Safety Gloves"	$20-$35
Pin, celluloid button, "The NEW GUARD, READY TO RIDE FOR FREEDOM," 1-1/4", with B, Aircraft, Auto, Motorcycle	$25-$35
Pin, celluloid button, "LET'S RIDE TOGETHER," 1", R/B, passenger tire	$25-$40
Pin, celluloid button, "PUERTO RICO CIVILIAN DEFENSE," 1-1/4", blue/white, "C Defense, Community of Damas"	$20-$30
Pin, celluloid button, "RAILROAD DEFENSE CORPS," 1-1/4", RWB, red keystone logo of "PA. Railroad"	$25-$35
Pin, celluloid button, "SALVAGE, Conservation Volunteer," 3/4", RWB	$20-$30
Pin, celluloid button, "STOP WASTE/HELP SAVE," 1-1/4", RWB, "Honor Award" for Conservation"	$20-$35

Item	**Value**
Ration Book Holder, 5" x 7", brown leather, gold U.S. National Seal	$20-$25
Ration Coupon, Coca-Cola Syrup Allotment, 1941	$5-$7
Seed Packs, "Victory Seeds," 4-1/2" x 3-1/4", Richfield, 1944 and 1945, each	$10-$15
Spotter's Dial, "Target Tokyo," "Wards Tip-top Bread," 1944	$20-$25
Stickers, "Donut Month" set of five, orange/black/white, 1941-1945	$45-$55
War Bond, $25, never cashed, 6-1/2" x 8-1/2", 1943	$85-$100

Pin/Sticker, "Gold for Dentistry," RWB/gold, 1942 ($20-$25 set).

Framed Photo, "U.S.A.," 8" x 10", RWB, all glass ($30-$40).

Booklet, "MAKE AND MEND FOR VICTORY," 10-1/2" x 7-1/2", RWB, Spool Cotton Co., 1942 ($5-$10).

Helmet, Air Raid Warden, white with red and white stripes in triangle on blue circle ($40-$50).

Ration Stickers, Automobile, Gasoline, 2-1/2" x 3-1/8", "A" black, "B" green, "C" red ($50-$65 set).

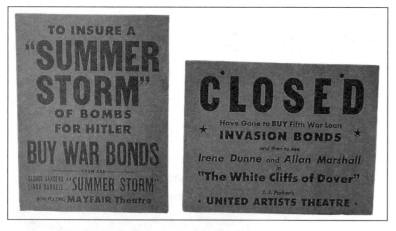

Signs, movie window, 8-1/2" x 11" ($30-$45 each).

Lantern, blackout type, black metal/reflective inner chamber/ candle holder/flip down front, PLECO, 1943 ($75-$100).

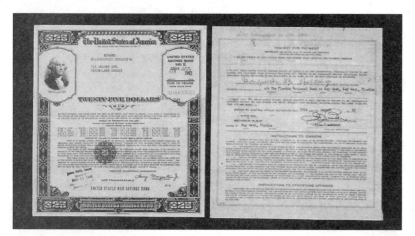

War Savings Bond, 7-1/2" x 8 -1/2", U.S. $25, reverse of U.S. $50 ($75-$100 each).

Coffee Maker, "JIFFY ONE CUPPER," three glass pieces/cloth filter, "Make Your Rationed Coffee Go Further" ($45-$55).

Sign, Window, "WE BOUGHT EXTRA WAR BONDS/6th WAR LOAN, 8" x 10", Uncle Sam with rifle running through the No. 6 ($25-$35).

Booklet, "HANDBOOK of CIVILIAN DEFENSE," Whitman Pub., 1942 ($15-$20).

Identification Badge Holder, DEFENSE WORKERS, on card it is 3-1/2" x 7", badge is 2-1/4" dia., value of badge on card ($30-$35); badge alone ($20-$25).

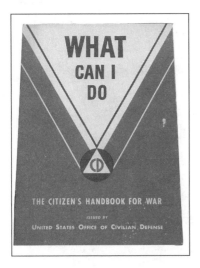

Booklet, "What Can I Do? the Citizen's Handbook for War," 1942 ($10-$15).

Booklet, "ARCHITECTURAL FORUM of CIVILIAN DEFENSE," 1942 ($10-$15).

Sign, "FOOD FOR VICTORY," 11" x 14", RWB, cardboard, USDA ($25-$35).

Pin/Patch, "Bundles for Blue Jackets," RWB/gold ($50-$65 set).

Booklet, *"500 Ways to Save in Your Home,"*
8-1/2" x 11", "It's Patriotic to Be Thrifty"
($15-$20).

Booklet, *"AERONAUTICS, AIRCRAFT*
SPOTTER'S GUIDE," issue #3, 6" x 9",
96 pages, 1942 ($20-$25).

Booklet, *"Coupon Cookery" RWB, by Prudence*
Penny ($15-$20).

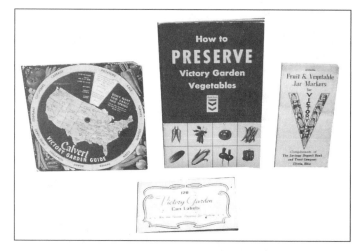

Booklets *($10-$20 each).*

Decal, *"GIVE TO THE USO," 5-3/4" x 4-1/2", RWB*
($20-$25).

Make-up, *"Stocking Silk," 2-1/2" x 2" x 1 -1/4", substi-*
tute for stockings. "Sun Valley Tan" ($75-$85).

Sign, *SALVAGE FOR VICTORY*
PROGRAM," 8", RWB ($20-$30).

Sign, air warden, 7" x 6", cardboard, "In Case of Disaster, War Action, or an Air Raid…" ($15-$20).

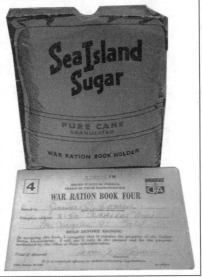

Ration Book/Holder, Sea Island Sugar holder and book ($15-$20).

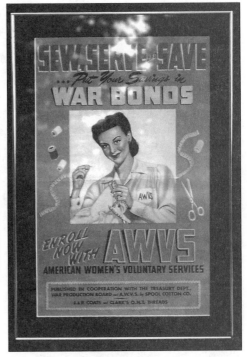

Poster, "Sew, Serve and Save," 21" x 31", "Enroll Now with AWVS, American Women's Volunteer Service" ($75-$95).

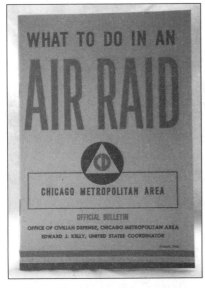

Booklet, "WHAT TO DO IN AN AIR RAID," Chicago, April 1942 ($10-$15).

Aircraft Spotters Dial, "Wards Tip-top Bread," 1943 ($10-$15).

Point Rationing Budget Book, 4-1/2" x 6", "Make Your Points Go Further!" ($5-$10).

Pin/Sticker, Red Cross Home Nursing, "Learn to Guard the Homefront," pin ($15-$20); sticker ($2-$3).

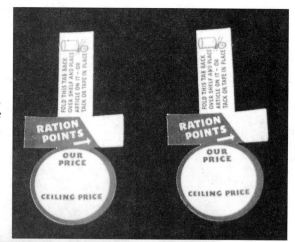

Tags, Ration Counter, 4-1/2" x 2", red/white ($5-$10 each).

Cheese Box, Kraft, 5" x 7-1/2", "Cheese Recipes for Wartime Meals" ($15-$20).

Milk Bottles ($45-$55 each).

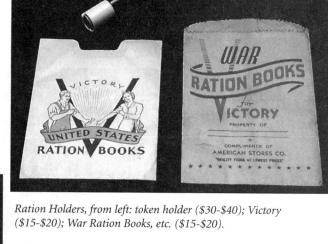

Ration Holders, from left: token holder ($30-$40); Victory ($15-$20); War Ration Books, etc. ($15-$20).

Postal Saving Stamp Booklets, 3-1/2" x 5-1/2", "UNITED STATES SAVINGS BONDS," 1942 ($125-$150 set).

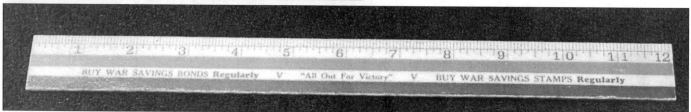

Ruler, "BUY WAR BONDS," 12" x 1-1/4", wooden, RWB, Newton Mfg. Co ($20-$25).

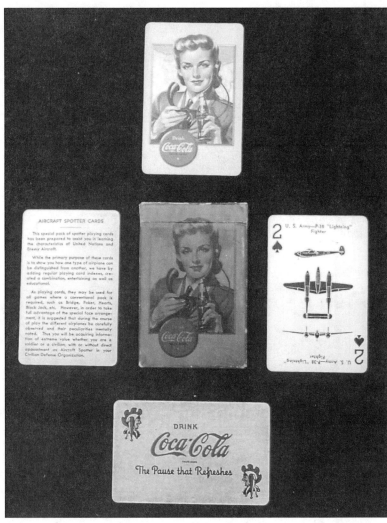

Spotter Cards, "Coca-Cola," woman with head set ($100-$125).

Window Sticker, 4-1/2" x 4", "VICTORY GARDEN" ($20-$25); canning label, 4" x 2", ($10-$15).

Badge, worker ID, 2" dia., "Standard Steel Spring Co." ($25-$30).

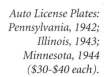

Auto License Plates: Pennsylvania, 1942; Illinois, 1943; Minnesota, 1944 ($30-$40 each).

Booklet, War Almanac, "America Strikes Back!", soldier with rifle, 1942 ($15-$20).

Catalog, "Paradise Seed Co., Premiums from Paradise," RWB, Paradise, PA ($15-$20).

Sign, window, "This Home Did It Again," 11" x 14", RWB, 6th War Loan, 1944 ($20-$30).

Tray, milk glass, "KEEP 'EM FLYING, Buy Another SAVINGS BOND TODAY," R/W ($20-$25).

Prints, framed, 8" x 10", kneeling helmeted soldier praying while Jesus watches over; and Sailor/Nurse/Soldier walking together, thermometer on frame, 6" x 8" ($20-$25 each).

Picture/Service Record Book, "His Service Record" ($40-$55 set).

Poster, "CAN ALL YOU CAN," 20" x 28", jar/vegetables, 1943 ($45-$55).

Booklet, "POWER FOR WAR," Electric Operating Co ($10-$15).

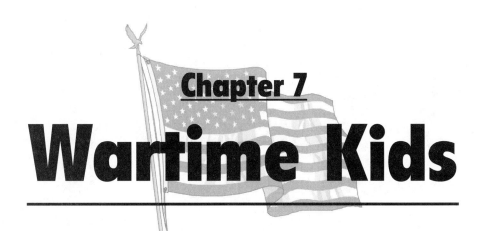

Chapter 7
Wartime Kids

Books

Item	Value
Book, *AIR FIGHTERS of AMERICA*, BLB, 1941	$25-$35
Book, *AMERICA IN ACTION, ON LAND, AT SEA, AND IN THE AIR*, Action Playbooks Inc., spiral, 1942	$50-$60
Book, *AMERICA'S ARMY*, 5-1/2" x 4-1/4", Rand McNally, 1942	$8-$10
Book, *DAY OF INFAMY*, 6" x 8-1/2", Walter Lord, 1942	$15-$20
Book, *Don O'Dare finds WAR*, Better Little Book, 1940	$15-$20
Book, *FIGHTING PLANES OF THE WORLD*, Random House, 1942	$15-$20
Book, *Fighting Yanks Around the World*, Thomas Penfield, Whitman Publishing Co., 1943	$20-$25
Book, *First Aid for the Injured*, Charles Scully, Whitman Publishing Co., hard cover, 1943	$10-$15
Book, *A Guide Book to the U.S. Army*, Fletcher Pratt, Whitman Publishing Co., hard cover, 1943	$10-$15
Book, *A Guide Book to the U.S. Navy*, Barry Bart & James Wallace, Whitman Publishing Co., hard cover, 1942	$10-$15
Book, *A Guide to Codes and Signals*, Gordon Peterson & Marshall McClintock, Whitman Publishing Co., hard cover, 1942	$10-$15
Book, *KEEP 'EM FLYING*, Better Little Book, 1943	$25-$35
Book, *LITTLE OSCAR'S FIRST RAID*, 8-3/4" x 7", Dodd, Mead & Co., 1944	$20-$25
Book, *Mother Goose Victory House*, American Crayon Co	$15-$20
Book, *Ray Land of the TANK CORPS*, giant tank running over enemy soldiers, Whitman Pub	$30-$40
Book, *Soldiers, Sailors, Fliers and Marines*, 9-1/4" x 7", Junior Books, 1943	$20-$25
Book, *The SECRETS OF RADAR*	$20-$25
Book, *Speed Douglas and the MOLE GANG*, Better Little Book, 1941	$25-$35
Book, *Uncle Sam's SKY DEFENDERS*, BLB, 1941	$25-$35
Book, *Vic Sands of the U.S., FLYING FORTRESS*, 4-1/2 x 3-1/2", Better Little Book. RWB, B-17	$25-$30
Book, *A WARTIME HANDBOOK FOR YOUNG AMERICANS*, 10-1/4" x 8", Frederick A. Stokes Co., 1942	$20-$30
Book, *WINGS of the U.S.A.*, Better Little Book, 1940	$15-$20
Magazine, *Children's Play Mate*, 9" x 6", A.R. Mueller Printing, 1944	$10-$15
Stamp Album, *FIGHTING SHIPS OF THE USA*, Whitman Pub., soft, 1942	$20-$30

How Boys and Girls Can Help Win the War, Uncle Sam with happy boy and girl, 10-1/2" x 7-1/2", Parents Magazine Press, NY, 1942 ($20-$25).

Capt. BEN DIX, 8-1/8" x 11", In Action with the Invisible Crew, Bendix Corp ($25-$30).

Battle Planes, Dell Pub., 1941 ($10-$15).

MODERN WARPLANES, Garden City Pub., 1942 ($15-$20).

Red Randall Over Tokyo, Red Randall at Pearl Harbor, Springboard to Tokyo, A Yankee Flier in Normandy ($15-$20 each).

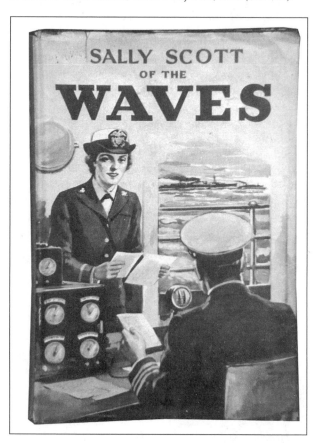

Sally Scott of the WAVES, dust jacket, Whitman Pub., 1943 ($15-$20).

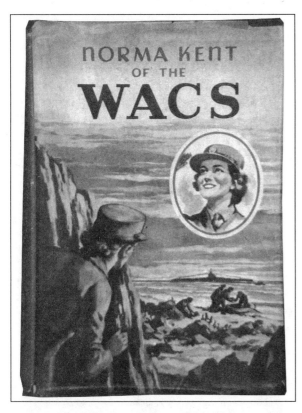

Norma Kent of the WACS, dust jacket, Whitman Pub., 1943 ($15-$20).

David Dawson on Convoy Patrol, Saalfield Pub., 1941 ($15-$20).

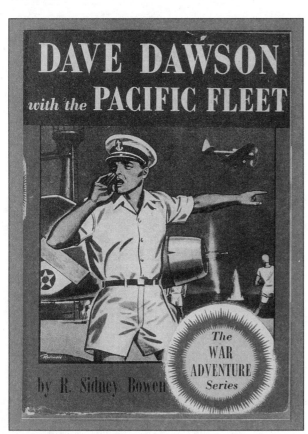

David Dawson with the Pacific Fleet, Saalfield Pub., 1941 ($15-$20 each).

SPITFIRE PILOT, dust jacket, Grosset and Dunlap, 1942 ($15-$20).

Punch Davis of the AIRCRAFT CARRIER, 348 pages, 1945 ($15-$20).

Allen Pike of the PARACHUTE SQUAD, Better Little Book, 1941 ($25-$35).

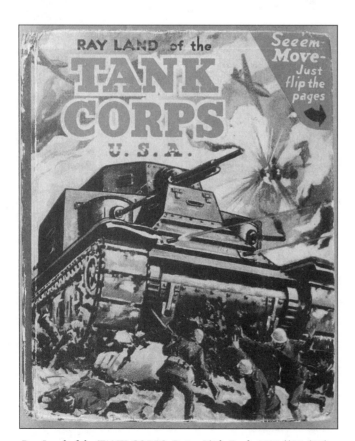

Ray Land of the TANK CORPS, Better Little Book, 1942 ($25-$35).

CONVOY PATROL, Better Little Book, 1942 ($25-$35).

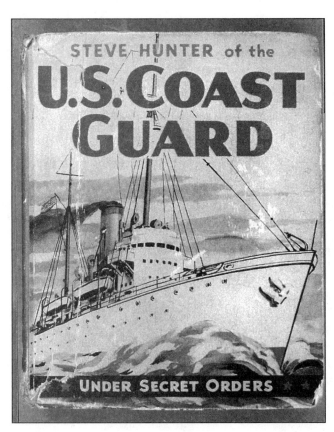

Steve Hunter of the U.S. Coast Guard, Better Little Book, 1942 ($25-$35).

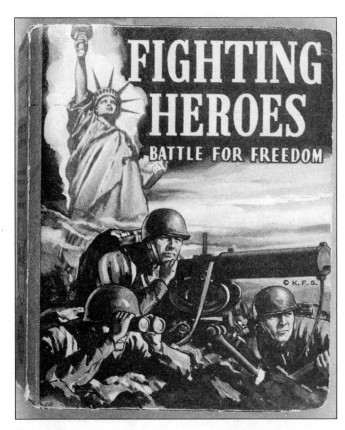

FIGHTING HEROES, Battle for Freedom, Better Little Book, 1943 ($35-$50).

Pilot Pete DIVE BOMBER, Better Little Book, 1941 ($25-$35).

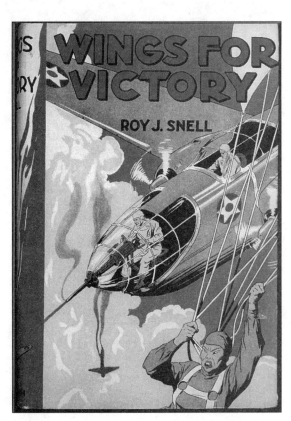

WINGS FOR VICTORY, 5-1/2" x 8-1/4", Goldsmith Pub., 1942 ($20-$25).

Barry Blake of the FLYING FORTRESS, 5-1/2" x 8",
Whitman Pub., 1943 ($25-$35).

FOREIGN SPIES, Doctor Doom and the Ghost Submarine,
BLB, 1941 ($25-$35).

Spike Kelly of the COMMANDOS, Whitman Pub., 1943 ($25-$35).

Comic Books

Item	Value
Capt. Marvel Jr., #11, Fawcett Pubs, 1942	$75-$85
Captain Midnight Secret Squadron, Book of Official Charts, Codes, Secrets, Ovaltine Pub., 1942	$150-$200
Complete War Novels, Western Fiction Pub., May 1943	$15-$20
Heroic Comics, No.25	$10-$15
How Boys and Girls Can Help Win the War, Dell Pub., 1942	$75-$100
I Was a Nazi Flier, German pilot's actual diary, Dell War Book, Dial Press, 1941	$40-$50
Rip Rider, Tops Comics, Consolidated Book Pub., 1944	$55-$150
Superman, #14, Jan/Feb 1942, DC	$2,000-$2,400
Superman, #34, May/June 1945, DC	$625-$750

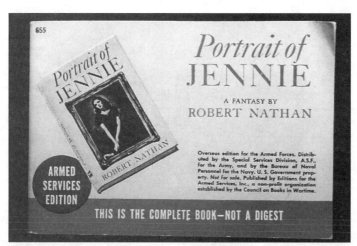

Portrait of Jennie, Armed Services Edition ($15-$20).

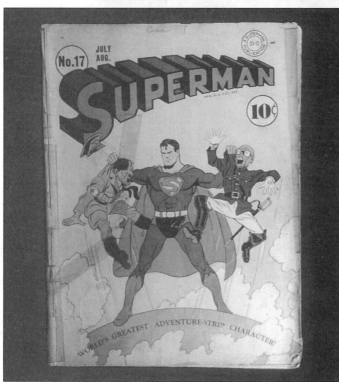

Superman, #17, July/Aug 1942, DC ($1,000-$1,350).

Superman, #13, Nov/Dec 1941, DC ($1,200-$1,500).

Superman, #18, Sept/Oct 1942, DC ($925-$1,200).

Superman, #26, Jan/Feb 1944, DC ($675-$850).

Superman, #20, Jan/Feb 1943, DC ($975-$1,250).

The Secret Voice, #1, American Features Syndicate, 1945 ($145-$165).

USA at War, Dunellen, 1942 ($40-$50).

Superman, #23, July/Aug 1943, DC ($725-$940).

Fighting Aces, Fictioneers, January 1944 ($20-$30).

Dare-Devil Aces, Popular Pub., May 1942 ($15-$20).

Dare Devil Aces, Popular Pub. December 1943 ($20-$30).

Army/Navy Flying Stories, Nedor Pub., Fall 1943 ($15-$20).

Draftie of the U.S. Army, Whitman Pub., 1943 ($25-$35)

Air War, Better Publications, Summer 1942 ($15-$20).

American Eagles, Better Publications, Spring 1943 ($15-$20).

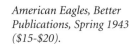

Figures

Item	Value
Lamp, Chalkware, boy in army uniform, 3" x 2-1/2", army and navy boys saluting on shade	$50-$75
Lamp, Chalkware, boy in navy uniform, 3" x 2-1/2", two boys and submarine on shade	$50-$75

Doll, Army officer, 6" x 3-3/4", celluloid, pinks/ greens ($50-$65).

Doll, U.S. Sailor, 8", soft ($35-$50).

Chalkware, female in uniform, 12-1/2" x 4-3/4" ($85-$100).

Doll, Army soldier, 12" x 6", saluting, cloth ($85-$100).

Doll, Army soldier, 13-1/3" x 4-1/2", cloth, full uniform ($85-$100).

Chalkware, WAC officer, 6-3/8" x 5-1/2", 1942 ($65-90).

Chalkware, "V" with saluting soldier in clouds," RWB ($45-$55).

Chalkware, Army soldier, 6-1/2" x 4", walking with helmet and rifle, multicolored, De Luxe Corp., WI ($35-$45).

Chalkware, female in uniform, 9" x 2-3/4" ($45-$55).

Chalkware, sailor, 13-3/4" x 6", blue sailor suit ($95-$120).

Chalkware, Uncle Sam, 15-1/2" x 4-1/2", no hat, rolling up sleeve, RWB ($135-$165).

Chalkware, eagle "God Bless America," 11" x 6", RWB ($80-$100).

Chalkware, "The Long Goodbye," 11" x 8-1/2", kissing couple wall hanging ($95-$115).

*Chalkware, "Uncle Sam" 15" high,
rolling up sleeves ($125-$150).*

*Chalkware, picture frame stand, 7-3/4" x 6", gold/brown soldier
standing with rifle, shield/ship ($65-$75).*

*Chalkware, picture frame stand, 7-3/4" x 6", gold/brown soldier standing
with rifle, shield/soldiers attacking/tank ($65-$75).*

Chalkware, picture frame stand, 7-3/4" x 6", gold/brown flier standing, shield/wings ($65-$75).

Chalkware, baby seated on bullet wearing army cap, 5" x 5-1/2", "Hatched in the USA" ($125-$150).

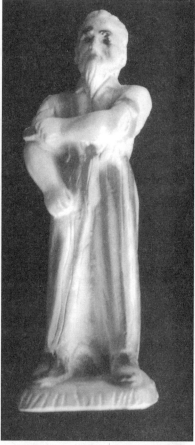

Chalkware, "Uncle Sam," 26" x 6", "It's Everyone's Fight," helmet and olive drab shirt, hands on hips ($325-$400).

Chalkware, soldier saluting, 14-1/2" x 4", class "A" uniform ($100-$125).

Chalkware, "Uncle Sam," 16" x 6", no hat, rolling up sleeves to fight ($225-$275).

*Chalkware, WAAC, saluting, 16"
high, WAAC inscribed on base,
Paoletti Bros ($100-$125).*

*Chalkware, soldier, full uniform, 15" high,
Pacinins Co. ($100-$125).*

*Chalkware, soldier, saluting, 15" high
($100-$125).*

*Figure, sailor, 10-1/2" x 3-1/2", paper/
pipe cleaners ($20-$30).*

*Figure, MacAuthur, 18-1/2" x 6", realistic
($275).*

Gum Cards

Gum Card Set #1: "AMERICA AT WAR," cards are 2-7/16" x 2-11/16", fronts have multicolor drawings/backs have titles and short text. Numbered 501-548, W.S. Company, 1942

Item	Value
512 U.S. Naval Attack at Marshall Islands	$7-$10
515 General Stillwell	$10-$15
529 Navy Tunnel at Corregidor	$7-$10
530 Stalin	$10-$15
534 Sinking Japs at Coral Sea	$7-$10
543 Machine Guns at Bataan	$7-$10

Flying Tigers in Burma ($10-$15).

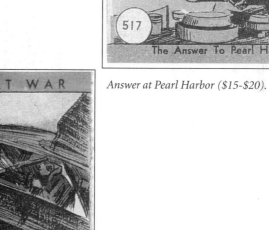

Answer at Pearl Harbor ($15-$20).

U.S. Planes Bomb Tokio ($10-$15).

Invasion of Europe ($15-$20).

Colin P. Kelly ($35-$45).

Gum Card Set #2: "ARMY, NAVY, AND AIR CORPS," cards are 2-3/8" x 2-11/16", fronts have multicolor drawings of war scenes, rouletted edges on 2 sides, backs carry short explanation. Numbered 601-648, W.S. Company, 1942

Item	Value
605 General Wainwright	$15-$20
622 Bombers Over the Pacific	$7-$10
639 General Marshall	$10-$15

General MacArthur at Corregidor ($20-$25).

President Roosevelt ($20-$25).

Gum Card Set #3: "COMMANDO-RANGER" cards, 2-1/2" x 2-3/4", "Pictogram" cards, red-blue "V" side panels, color artwork on front, gray backs with green, blue or black print, numbered 1-70, W.H. Brady, 1942

Item	Value
23 Courageous Lieut. Col. Raft	$15-$20
44 Overpowering Jap Sub Crew	$7-$10
48 Helpless Hitlerite in Head-Hold	$25-$35
53 Vital Dive Bomber	$7-$10
57 Dive Bombing Nazi Navy	$7-$10
61 Beating Up Axis Bullies	$7-$10
69 Invaders Board Troop Transport	$7-$10
70 Dog Heroes in Action	$7-$10

Armored Car Annihilates Nazis ($7-$10).

Gum Card Set #4: "HEROES OF PEARL HARBOR," cards are 1-7/8" x 3", red and blue with white accents, 2 cards were printed on front and back panels of single candy box, unnumbered (8 cards), Candyland Co. Brooklyn, NY, 1942

Item	Value
3 Capt. Colin Kelly Jr.	$75-$100
4 Rear Admiral Isaac Cambell Kidd	$50-$75
5 2nd Lieutenant Louis G. Mesiene	$50-$75
6 Private Robert B. Niedzwiecki	$50-$75

Lieutenant Hans C. Christiansen ($50-$75).

Private William M. Northway ($50-$75).

Private Ralph S. Smith ($50-$75).

Private Elmer W. South ($50-$75).

Gum Card Set #5: "UNCLE SAM & HOME DEFENSE," cards are 2-1/2" x 3-1/8", 2 separate subsets, numbered 1-96, multicolor art scenes from 4 different service branches; Army, Navy, Air Force, Marines and have a value of from $15-$20 each. Vivid illustrations of military preparedness for hostilities and overseas warfare cards numbered 97-144 depicts activities of civilian sector and are the most desired cards by homefront collectors today with a value of from $125-$150 each! In excellent condition. Published by Gum Inc., 1942

Item	Value
1 You're in the Army Now	$15-$20
38 Flight Instruction	$15-$20
41 Gunnery in the Air Corps	$15-$20
66 Machine Gun Practice	$15-$20
71 the Bombardier	$15-$20
74 Guard	$15-$20
90 Marine Sky Troops	$15-$20
96 Night Bomber	$15-$20

Field Artillery ($15-$20).

Destroyer Duty ($15-$20).

Home Guard Rifle Practice ($125-$150).

Auxiliary Coast Guard ($125-$150).

Item	**Value**
97 The Office of Civilian Defense	$125-$150
103 Children's Duties	$125-$150
104 Enlisting Home Guard	$125-$150
106 Spot Wardens	$125-$150
107 Medical Corps	$125-$150
108 Drivers Corps	$125-$150
110 Ammeter Radio Station Volunteers	$125-$150
111 Civilian Information About Bombs	$125-$150
112 Test Blackout	$125-$150
113 Protecting Windows and Doors	$125-$150
114 Civilian Type Gas Masks	$125-$150
115 Gas "Decontamination	$125-$150
116 Home Shelter Room	$125-$150
117 Steel Shelter	$125-$150
118 Public Shelter	$125-$150
119 Civilian Pilot Reserve	$125-$150
120 Keep 'em Flying	$125-$150

Bomb Squad ($125-$150).

Light Rescue Party ($125-$150).

Heavy Rescue Party ($125-$150).

Pigeon Raising for Defense ($125-$150).

Item	Value
121 Control and Report Centers	$125-$150
122 The Aircraft Warning Net	$125-$150
123 "Hale" America	$125-$150
124 Family Unit	$125-$150
125 Individual Defense Incendiary Bombs	$125-$150
126 Lightning Supervision	$125-$150
127 Dispersing School Children	$125-$150
128 Fire Watcher	$125-$150
130 Training First Air Instructors	$125-$150
131 First Aid Stations	$125-$150
134 Rescue Trucks	$125-$150
135 Factory Protection Squads	$125-$150
136 Use of Portable Fire Pump	$125-$150
137 Mobile Food Units	$125-$150
138 Road Repair Crew	$125-$150
139 Demolition Crew	$125-$150
140 Emergency Food and Housing	$125-$150
141 Preventing Disease	$125-$150
142 Guarding Water Supplies	$125-$150
144 Women Fliers in Defense	$125-$150

Gum Card Set #6: "VICTORY," cards are 1-7/8" x 3", 12 candy-box cards, multicolor, servicemen of specific ranks inside a large "V" and Morse code, red and yellow background. Victory Gum, 1941

Item	Value
1. Unknown	
2. United States General	$40-$50
3. United States Corporal	$40-$50
4. United States Midshipman	$40-$50

United States General ($40-$50).

United States Midshipman ($40-$50).

Item	Value
5. United States Colonel	$40-$50
6. United States Sailor	$40-$50
7. United States West Point Cadet	$40-$50
8. United States Buck Private	$40-$50
9. United States Lieutenant	$40-$50
10. United States Navy Captain	$40-$50
11. United States Sergeant	$40-$50
12. United States Marine	$40-$50

United States West Point Cadet ($40-$50).   *United States Buck Private ($40-$50).*

Gum Card Set #7: "WAR GUM," cards are 2-1/2" x 3-1/8", numbered 1-132, full color illustrations depict bravery of U.S. and Allied serviceman and leaders. Captions on front of cards, descriptions on back. Cards issued in 6 different wrappers (rare). Published by Gum, Inc., 1941-1942

Wrappers only (no cards)

Item	Value
Pearl Harbor	$500-$550
Wake Island	$525-$575
Philippines	$550-$600
Indo-China/Malays	$600-$650
Soldier (Green)	$600-$675
Soldier (Orange)	$675-$725

Cards

Item	Value
1 Franklin Delano Roosevelt	$35-$40
15 Winston Churchill	$20-$25
19 General George Marshall	$15-$20
21 General Sir Archibald P. Wavell	$20-$25

Defense of Wake Island ($15-$20).

General Douglas MacArthur ($30-$35).

Midway Island Defies the Japs ($15-$20).

Sailorman's Gun Alone ($15-$20).

Item	Value
42 Admiral Chester W. Nimitz	$20-$25
55 "ACE" LT. Edward O'Hare	$20-$25
71 Doolittle Receives Congressional Medal	$25-$30
76 Brigadier General Chennault of the Tigers	$25-$30
90 R.A.F. Scourges Hamburg	$15-$20
101 Miss Lee Ya-Chipang, China's First Female Pilot	$15-$20
104 Victor Talalikhin, Russian Air Hero	$15-$20
116 Captain George "Ed" Kiser	$15-$20
117 Wilkie Visits World Battlegrounds	$15-$20
132 Heroic Defense at Stalingrad	$15-$20

Gum Card Set #8: "WAR SCENES," cards are 2-1/4" x 2-11/16", multicolored art on front/backs are numbered 101-148 and printed in either blue, lavender or black inks with descriptions, MP and Co. "Made in USA," 1943

Item	Value
102 Curtis Dive Bomber SB2C-1	$10-$15
119 Churchill Decorating Commandos	$15-$20
122 U-boat Sunk by Planes	$10-$15
125 Destroyers Attacking Midway Island	$10-$15
127 U. S. Submarines in Coral Sea	$10-$15
132 Admiral Ernest J. King	$10-$15
140 Brig. General James A. Doolittle	$10-$15
143 Torpedo and Dive Bombers at Midway	$10-$15
148 Admiral Nimitz, U. S. N. Pacific Chief	$15-$20

General MacArthur in Australia ($20-$25).

U. S. S. Saratoga and Bombers ($10-$15).

Naval Base at Pearl Harbor ($10-$15).

Sinking Jap Carrier at Midway ($10-$15).

Models

Item	Value
Battleship, paper, in envelope. 9" x 7", Reed/Associates, Chicago	$15-$20
Howitzer 105 mm, 3-5/8" x 12", balsa wood, R/W, Ace Model Shop	$25-$35
Jeep/Anti-Aircraft Gun, 5" x 13", b&w, Ace Model Shop	$30-$40
Plane, Kellogg's Pep Cereal, punch-out Hellcat	$15-$20
Plane, Wheaties Cereal, punch-out, Jap Zero	$25-$30
Plane, Wheaties Cereal, punch-out, P-40	$25-$30
Torpedo Boat, 3-1/2" x 15-1/2", Comet	$35-$45

All Star Jeep, 14-1/4" x 6-1/4", RWB, Kempro Co., IL, 1944 ($65-$75).

War Tank, 9-1/2" x 4", Marvel Mfg. Co., 1940 ($35-$45); Comet, 15-1/2" x 3-1/2", Keep Em Flying Series ($35-$45).

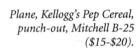

Plane, Kellogg's Pep Cereal, punch-out, Mitchell B-25 ($15-$20).

Jr. War Models, 9-1/2" x 12", Jeep and Gun ($35-$45).

Construction set, Yank-E-Tanks, punch-out, 13" x 16", W.E. MacLaren Co., 1943 ($150-$175).

"AIR DEFENSE," Whitman ($100-$125).

DESTROYER, 3-1/2" x 15-1/2", Comet ($35-$45).

Playbooks

Item	Value
Activity Book, "Cut and Stick," 9" x 12", Our Army and Navy in Action, Merrill	$35-$45
Book, Pop-Up, "The Victory March," Walt Disney, 8" x 10", 1942	$85-$100
Coloring Book, "SPOT PLANES," 10" x 13-1/2", Merrill	$60-$75
Coloring Book, "Victory Coloring Book," Saalfield Publishing Co., 1943	$30-$35
Paint Book, "Action Paint Book," Samuel Lowe Co., 1943	$20-$25
Paint book, "Victory," 11" x 15", boy in Army uniform looking over "V", Whitman Publishing, 1942	$25-$30
Play-Book, "America in Action," 11" x 13-3/4", on land/sea/air, sliding wheels and pop-ups, Action Playbooks, 1942	$30-$40
Paper Dolls, "AIR, LAND and SEA", Saalfield Pub	$125-$150
Paper Dolls, "ARMY NURSE and Doctor," Merrill	$125-$150
Paper Dolls, "NAVY GIRLS," Merrill	$125-$150
Paper Dolls, "VICTORY," Merrill	$125-$150
Paper Doll Kit, "Our NURSE Nancy," 9" x 10-1/2", Whitman Pub	$50-$75
Paper Doll Kit, "Our SOLDIER Jim," 9" x 10-1/2", Whitman Pub	$50-$75
Stamp Album, "War Album of Victory Battles," 24 stamps, General Mills Inc., 1945	$20-$25
Stamp Album, "War Planes of the World," Best Foods Inc., 1943	$20-$25
Stamp Book, "Fighting Ships of the U.S.A.," Whitman Publishing, 1943	$20-$25
Stamp Album, "Sky Heroes," 4" x 8-3/4", holds 20 stamps of heroic pilots, Roscoe Parkinson, 1944	$75-$100

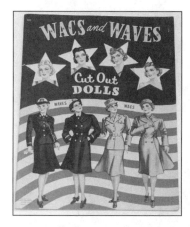

Paper Dolls, "WACS and WAVES," Whitman ($125-$150).

Coloring Book, "Big Boom," 15" x 10-1/2", Merrill Pub., 1942 ($35-$45).

Coloring Book, "Fighting Yanks," 14" x 11", Saalfield Pub. ($35-$45).

Coloring Book, "HI SAILOR," 10-3/4" x 8-1/2", Saalfield Pub., 1944 ($25-$30).

Paper Dolls, "STAGE DOOR CANTEEN," Saalfield Pub. ($100-$125).

Paper Dolls, "Bride and Groom," Merrill ($50-$75).

Playbooks ($30-$45 each).

Playthings

Tattoos, "Victory Tattoos," 11" x 9", temporary tattoos on R/W card ($20-$30).

Clothes Pins, "Dolly Pins," 2-1/2" x 4-1/4", RWB ($5-$10).

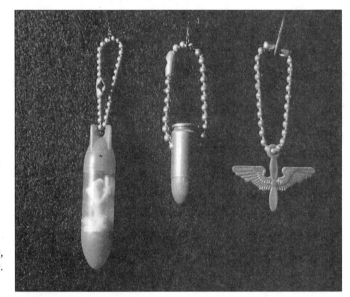

Key Chains, plastic: naked girl in bomb ($20-$25), bullet ($5-$7), wing and prop ($10-$15).

Booklet, "Left Overs," 9" x 7-1/4", G.I. Cartoon Book, Art Litho Co., TX, 1945 ($15-$20).

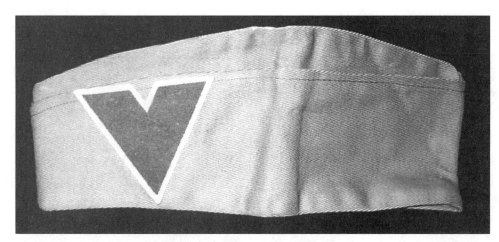

Cap, high school "Victory Corp. General's," gray/red felt "V," Lowe's and Campbell Athletic Goods ($35-$45).

Arm Band, "Junior Commando," Philadelphia Inquirer, White Printing on Red Felt ($20-$25).

Patch, "Junior Commando," "Burbank," gold stitching on white, "JC" on black shield on pilot's wings ($15-$20).

Patch/Pin, "Junior Commando," black printing on white background ($25-$30 set).

Soap, figural bars in display container, 11" x 7-1/8", Soldier, Nurse, Wave, WAC, each 4" to 4-1/2" high, "We Love Our Flag, Our Country Too, The Stars, Red, White and Blue," Fun-E-Sope, Tre-Jur, NY ($100-$125).

Soap, figural bars in display container, 8-1/4" x 7-1/2", WAC, Uncle Sam, "Hall of Fame," "I save my pennies, nickels and dimes, I've given up many of my good times…," Fun-E-Sope, Tre-Jur, NY ($65-$75).

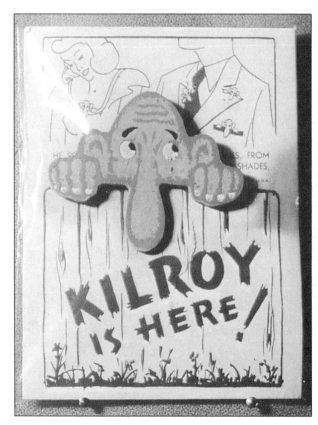

Soap, figural bars, "Defenders of the Bath," "The Soapy Yanks," marine and pilot ($30-$35 each).

Clip, "Kilroy is Here," 3" x 5", cut out of Kilroy that clips on clothing, on card ($75-$90).

Soap, figural bars in display container, 11-3/4" x 4-3/4", 3 sailors with large ears, "Meet You in Berlin, Meet You in Tokio, Meet You in Rome," Fun-E-Sope, Tre-Jur, NY ($75-$100).

Soap, figural bars in display container, 7-1/4" x 6", 2 soldiers with rifles and caps, "Army Recruiting Station…," Fun-E-Sope, Tre-Jur, NY ($65-$75).

Paint Set, "The AMERICAN Rangers," American Crayon Co. ($65-$75).

Gun, Coast Defense, 7-1/4" x 8-1/4", shoots pegs, Baldwin Mfg. ($90-$100).

Pin, cello button, "100% for Democracy," 1-1/4", Bill Boyd as Hopal-ong Cassidy, b&w ($100-$125).

Coasters, set of 4, heavy paper, 3-1/2" dia., RWB, soldier/marine/flier/warden ($50-$65 set).

Rings, metal ($25-$45 each).

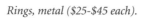

Ice Cream Tops, 2-3/4", war scenes, Dixie's Ice Cream ($25-$35 set).

Toys

Children played an important role on the homefront. They collected scrap materials for the war effort and joined their schools' Victory Clubs. Iron, tin, aluminum, paper and even cooking fat was collected and converted into war material. At school, kids would often save their allowance and skip lunch to buy 10 and 25 cent War Bond Stamps that could be used to buy a $25 Saving Bond for $18.25.

In addition, more than 100,000 model airplanes, ships and fighting vehicles were built by wartime kids for use by the military to train soldiers and civilians in distinguishing between Allied and Axis equipment. Boy and Girl Scouts also helped at the USO (United Service Organization), veteran's hospitals and the Red Cross as well as promoting the sale of U.S. War Bonds.

Games

Item	Value
Dexterity Game, "Trap the Jap in Tokyo," Modern Novelties Inc. Ohio, 1941	$45-$65
Game, "AIM and FIRE," 6-1/2" x 9-1/4", Alliance Game Co., 1943	$35-$45
Game, "Bild a Set," 10-1/2" x 14", Army and Navy punch-out set, 1943	$125-$150
Game, "BLACKOUT KIT," 15-1/4" x 9-1/2", Vernon Co., 1942	$65-$75
Game, "The Bomber," 3-1/4" x 4-1/4", dexterity game in box with glass front	$50-$60
Game, "Bomb-Site," 21-1/2" x 23-1/2", dart board representing Japanese targets	$125-$150
Game, "BUILD-YOUR-OWN-U.S. DEFENSE," 14" x 10-3/4", Standard Toykraft Products	$55-$65
Game, "LAND and SEA," 11" x 11", War Games, Samuel Lowe Co., 1941	$35-$45
Game, "Lone Ranger's BLACK OUT KIT," "It Glows in the Dark," 3-1/2" x 9-1/2", 1942	$45-$65
Game, "Salute," 9-1/2" x 18-1/4", Selchow and Righter	$35-$45
Game, "SLID'EM, TANK ATTACK PUZZLE," 4" x 6", fold out, Electric Corp. of America, 1942	$25-$35
Game, "Stand Up Soldiers in Action" 7-1/4" x 10", All Fair	$45-$55
Game, "Victory," 6" x 9", "Bingo Game of War Heroes," H.J. Millar, 1942	$30-$40
Game, "VICTORY BOMBER, POOSH-M-UP," 12-1/2" x 22", Wood/Fiberboard, Northwestern Products, MO	$65-$85
Game, "VICTORY Playing Cards"	$50-$65
Punch Board, "BIG BATTLE PUNCH GAME," 9" x 6-1/2", W.H. Brady Co.	$25-$30

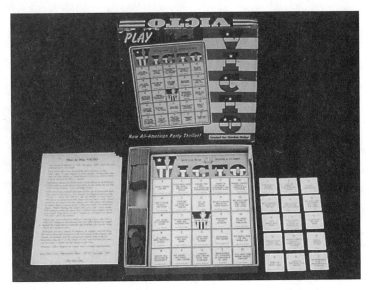

Game, "VICTO," 8-1/4" x 8-3/4", Spare-Time Corp, 1943 ($45-$55).

Item	**Value**
Punch board, "You're in the Army Now," 9-1/2" x 8-1/2", Hamilton Manufacturing Co	$85-$100
Puzzle, "World Map," U.S. Finishing and Mfg. Co., Chicago, 1943	$35-$50
Puzzles, "VICTORY Series and Leading American Artist Series," 8" x 11", J.S. Publishing Co., Saalfield Publishing Co	$30-$40
Target Game, "Bomber Ball," Game Makers, Long Island City NY, 1942	$150-$185
Target Game, "Direct Hit," 16" x 19", contains wooden airplane that drops darts on target, Northwestern Products, 1945	$125-$150
Target Game, "SMASH THE AXIS," Colorgraphic, Inc., Chicago, 1943	$100-$125
Target Game, "Victory Bomber," 10-1/2" x 6-3/4", Whitman Publishing Co	$65-$75

Game, "Spot-A-Plane," 20-1/4" x 10-1/4", Toy Creations, 1942 ($35-$45).

Game, "Put the Yanks in Berlin,"
Modern Novelties Inc. ($45-$55).

Game, "SPY," 14" x 10", All-Fair Games ($35-$45).

Game, "War Bingo," 6-1/2" x 9-3/4", Gotham Sales Co., 1942 ($35-$45).

Game, *"Squadron Scramble,"* 2-1/2" x 3-1/2", Brown Fighter Plane, RWB ($20-$30).

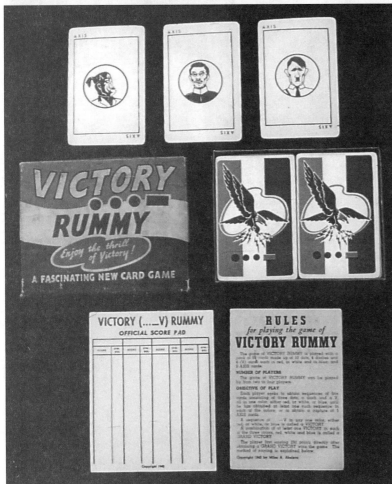

Game, *"At Ease,"* 4-1/2" x 6-1/4", RWB, Reginald Leister ($20-$25).

Game, *"VICTORY RUMMY,"* 4" x 5", RWB ($40-$45).

Game, "Bombs Away!", 18" x 18", dart board and bombsight, Toy Creations; and Eagle Bombsight, 9" x 4-1/2" x 2-1/4", Toy Creations ($75-$90 each).

Punch Board, toy soldier, stand-up, paper, 7-1/4" x 10", "Choice of Premiums," uniformed soldier with "Punch Outs" on back pack ($45-$50).

Card Game, "SABOTAGE," 4" x 5", Anderson and Sons, 1943 ($40-$45).

Playing Cards, "VICTORY," Double Deck, 4" x 5", Arco Playing Card Co. ($100-$125).

Game, "Ranger Commandos," 15" x 11", RWB, Parker Bros, 1944 ($55-$65).

Game, "Sink the Ship," 6-3/4" x 11-3/4", "Protect American Waters from the Enemy," Transogram Co. 1942 ($55-$65).

Game, "Jeep Patrol," 6-3/4" x 10", Lido Toy Co. ($35-$45).

Game, "Bomber Attack," 12" x 16", Fight the Enemy," Advanced Games, Inc., 1942 ($100-$125).

Game, "Flag," 11" x 17", The U.S. Flag Association, Parker Bros, 1943 ($45-$55).

Game, "Sea Raider," 8" x 16", "For Young Admirals," Parker Bros. ($35-$45).

Game, "Conflict," 10-1/2" x 20", Parker Bros ($75-$95).

Game, "Blockade," 16-1/4" x 22-1/4", "A Game for Armchair Admirals," Corey Games, 1941 ($75-$95).

Game, "Battle Checkers," 15-1/2" x 15-1/2", "Beat the Axis," Penmen, 1942 ($75-$95).

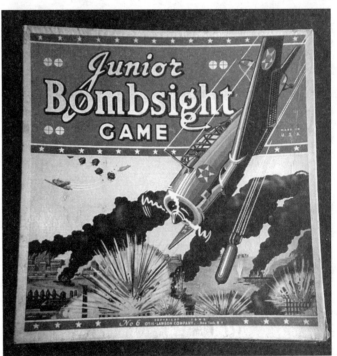

Game, JUNIOR AIR RAID WARDEN SET ($175-$200).

Game, "Junior Bombsight," 15-1/2" x 16", Otis-Lawson Co., 1942 ($150-$175).

Game, "BATAAN, the Battle of the Philippines," 9-1/2" x 19", Milton Bradley ($75-$85).

Game, "TRADE WINDS," Milton Bradley ($100-$125).

Game, "FERRY COMMAND," 16" x 21" ($125-$145).

Game, "Bo-Lem Ova," 13-3/4" x 19-1/2", bowling game, Kindred Co. ($175-$225).

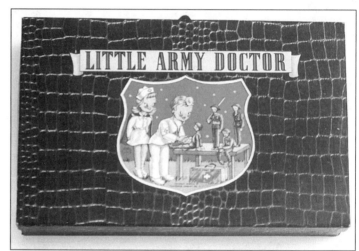

Game, "LITTLE ARMY DOCTOR," Transogram ($125-$150).

Game, "Bomb the Jap off the Map!" 16" x 16", dart board, plywood, RWB ($85-$100).

Game, "BLACKOUT," 15-1/2" x 21", Today's Game of Thrills, Milton Bradley, second version ($75-$85).

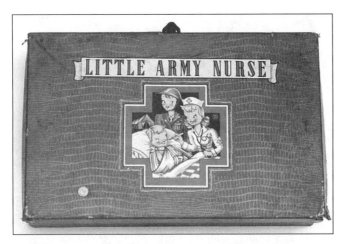

Game, *"LITTLE ARMY NURSE," Transogram ($100-$125).*

Game, *"BOMBER ATTACK," Fight the Enemy, Advanced Game Co. ($100-$125).*

Game, *"DIRECT HIT," Northwestern Products St. Louis ($225-$275).*

Game, *"CARGO for VICTORY," All-Fair Game ($75-$100).*

Game, *"INVASION," Gano Games Co. ($60-$75).*

Game, *"ARMY RAIDERS VICTORY UNIT," Warren Paper Products ($125-$150).*

Puzzles, "OUR DEFENDERS PUZZLES," 12" x 16-1/2", 3 puzzles, Saml. Gabriel and Sons ($55-$65 each).

Puzzles, "Patriotic Puzzles," The Yanks in Action on Land, Sea and Air, Transogram ($35-$45).

Game, "Trap a Sap," 3-1/4" x 4-1/4", dexterity game, glass front, shows Japanese Zero ($45-$55).

Game, "Keep 'em Rolling," 3-1/4" x 4-1/4", dexterity game, glass front, Military Trucks ($50-$60).

Game, "Atomic Bomb," 3-1/4" x 4-1/4", dexterity game, glass front, Atom Bomb, Fred-Alan Novelties, 1945 ($65-$75).

Game, "Ration Board," 10-1/4" x 20-1/4", Jayline Mfg., 1943 ($85-$100).

Puzzles, "Army and Navy Combat," 8-1/2" x 10-1/2", 4 puzzle set ($35-$45 for set).

Game, "Tin Fish Away," Submarine, Cibert Mfg., 1942 ($50-$75).

Game, "FLAGSHIP," board game, Games of Fame, Westfield, MA, 1944 ($50-$75).

Marbles, "VICTORY," 4" x 3-1/2", RWB ($25-$30).

Game, "LIBERTY," flag game, E.E. Fairchild Corp ($20-$30).

Game, "SQUADRON INSIGNIA," Navy Aircraft, E.E. Fairchild Corp ($40-$50).

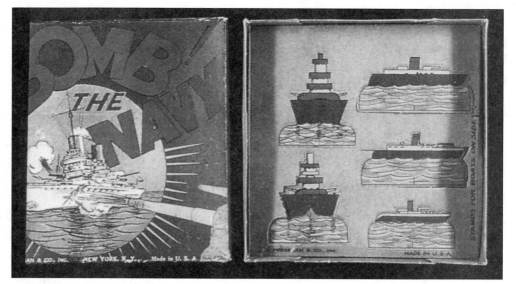

Game, target, "BOMB THE NAVY,"
Pressman and Co. NY, 1942 ($35-$50).

Puzzle, "FIGHTERS for FREEDOM," 8" x 11",
RWB, Whitman Pub. ($30-$40).

Puzzle, Solitaire, "Put Hitler in the Dog
House," Zen, Bridgeport, Conn, 1942 ($45-
$60).

Item	Value
Airplane, folded paper, 11" x 12-1/4", RWB, L. Schilling Co. N.Y.	$15-$20
Building Set, "Midgies SEABEES Construction Set," "A Complete SEABEES Unit," Jaymar, 1945	$75-$95
Crayon Holder, "Keep'em Flying" Crayons, 8 " x 5-1/2", A Gold Medal Toy	$35-$45
Clicker Gun, cardboard, 8" long, photo of MacArthur on grip, ON TO VICTORY	$25-$35
Game, SQUADRON INSIGNIA, navy aircraft, E. Fairchild Corp	$40-$50
Gun, Coast Defense, wood/tin, 7-1/4" x 8-1/4", shoots dowels, Baldwin Mfg.	$90-$100
Paint Box, "Kopy Kat," 4" x 10", red/picture of bomber, American Crayon Co. Ohio	$25-$35
Phone, WALKIE-TALKIE COMBAT PHONE, 8" x 3", Gung Ho	$45-$55
Pin, celluloid, "Junior Commando," 1-1/4", b&w, boy in helmet	$25-$45
Pin, celluloid, "Main Street Commando," 2-1/4", RWB, blue lettering on red "V"	$25-$40
Pin, celluloid, "Official Aluminum Collector, 1-1/4", RWB	$25-$35
Pin, celluloid, "Tin and Paper Commando," 1-1/4" red/white, "Collector of Scarce Wartime Materials"	$20-$35
Plane, "Blow-A-Plane," 10-1/2" x 10-1/2", paper, CTC	$30-$40
Searchlight, U.S. Army Searchlight, 4-1/2" x 12-1/2", MOD-AC	$35-$45
Tank, pull toy, 10" x 5", RWB, Cass Toys	$35-$50
Tank, VICTORY TANK, 8-1/2" x 4" x 3-1/2", Wood. Richard Appel	$50-$65
Toy Planes, WINGS AWAY, Lido Toy Corp. NY, 1942	$150-$175
Ukulele, wood, 21" x 6-3/4", RWB, planes, eagle, "V," by Regal	$1,000-$1,200
Whistle, Plastic with "V" and "…-", white	$20-$25
Wings, metal pinback, AMERICAN BOY JUNIOR PILOT, 2-3/4 x 5/8", gold, paper inscription in RWB, "Keep 'Em Flying"	$20-$25
Wings, metal pinback, "Junior Air Warden," 2-3/4" x 5/8", circular paper inscription in RWB, "Civil Defense"	$20-$25
Wings, metal pinback, "Junior Air Warden," 1-3/4", RWB, brass, enameled	$35-$50

Toy Plane, RAPID FIRE PURSUIT, from a target game, 9-1/2" wingspan, Gotham Pressed Steel Corp ($100-$125).

Target, 5-3/4" x 6-1/2", plane, tanks, Jeep, trucks and soldier, metal ($20-$30).

Trick, "Buzzer" pack of Lucky Strike Greens, key wind ($75-$100).

Reverse of "Buzzer" pack.

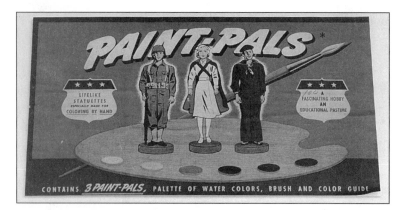

Paint Set, "Paint-Pals," soldier/nurse/sailor ($125-$150).

Periscope, "Commando Scope," 14" x 6" x 2", wood, Minneapolis ($45-$55).

Plane Set, "Victory Squadron," 6" x 8", three planes on display card, Irwin ($20-$30).

Tattoos, ACTION, 5-1/2" x 6", 48 tattoos, soldier/Tommy Gun ($25-$40).

Tank, wooden, 9-1/2" x 6-1/2", makes noise when rolled, olive drab green, Toy Craft ($55-$65).

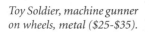

Toy Soldier, machine gunner on wheels, metal ($25-$35).

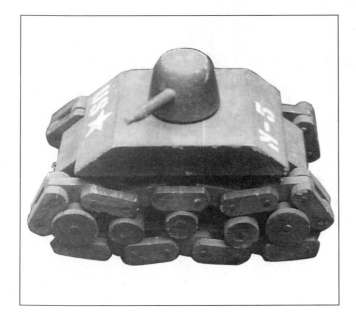

Tank, "N-5, U.S.," 6-1/2" x 5", x 4", wooden ($65-$85).

Tank, Tin Wind-Up, 9-1/2" x 6", sparkling side guns, camouflaged, rubber tracks, Marx ($200-$225).

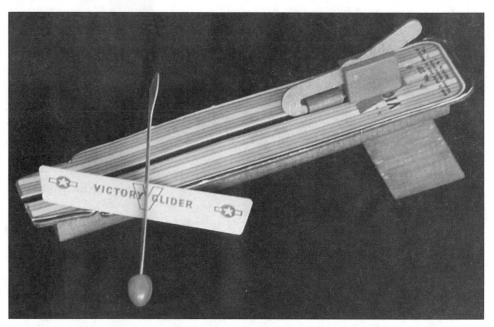

Viewer, MOVIE VIEWS OF UNCLE SAM'S U.S. ARMY, 7" x 9", contains movie viewer and 3 films ($75-$95).

Toy Gun, SUPER DEFENSE, Paper Buster Gun, 5-3/4" x 1/2", in box, Langson Mfg. Co. ($75-$90).

Rubber Band Plane Launcher, 10-1/2" x 3", shoots cardboard glider, Baldwin Mfg. Co. ($45-$55).

Rifle, Victory "Tommy Gun," 17-1/2" x 4", label RWB, natural wood ($85-$115).